MOUNTAIN HOME

Tales of Seeking a Family Life
in Harmony With Nature

Adolf Hungry Wolf

Canadian Caboose Press

For Further Reading:

SHADOWS OF THE BUFFALO
A Family Odyssey among the Indians
> By Adolf and Beverly Hungry Wolf. The story of two young people from very different backgrounds coming together in search of a deeply spiritual culture whose last practitioners were on the verge of dying out in the 1960's and 70's.

LETTERS FROM CUBA
Simple Living with Vintage Cars, Old Trains & Friendly People
> Written and photographed by Adolf Hungry Wolf during several extended journeys through the island of Cuba with individual members of his family in the 1990's, a time of great social change.

Also by Adolf Hungry Wolf:
- TEACHINGS OF NATURE
- GOOD MEDICINE COLLECTION
- INDIAN TRIBES OF THE NORTHERN ROCKIES
- THE BLOOD PEOPLE
- OFF ON A WILD CABOOSE CHASE
- RAILS IN THE CANADIAN ROCKIES
- RAILS IN THE MOTHER LODE
  and many more....

For a complete listing, write to:
Canadian Caboose Press, Box 844, Skookumchuck,
British Columbia, V0B 2E0, Canada

Front Cover: Part of a painting by Albert Bierstadt from the Glenn E. Nielson Collection in the Whitney Gallery of Western Art, Cody, Wyoming.

Canadian Cataloguing in Publication Data
Hungry Wolf, Adolf, 1944
Mountain Home
ISBN 0-920698-54-9
1. Hungry Wolf, Adolf, 1944- 2. Outdoor life -- Rocky Mountains Canada,
Canadian (B.C. and Alta.) 4. Rocky Mountains, Canadian (B.C. and Alta.) --
Biography. * I. Title.
FC219.H86 1996   971.1'04'092 C96-910644-0
F1090.H86 1996

Contents

Introduction

A treasured memory in our household is that of waking up around daybreak on cold and icy mornings back when our four children were still small, then snuggling together at one of the cabin windows to watch in silence as a herd of elk grazed peacefully outside on the snow covered grasses of our meadow. The only sounds were the occasional dull thumping of pointed hooves whenever they hit the frozen ground while pawing down through deep snow, along with constant munching as the golden-brown, pony-sized animals chewed on dried grasses, their steaming breaths swirling around mouths and nostrils, making us snuggle all the more tightly together. The highlight of these sessions usually came when one or more of the elk suddenly noticed us behind our window, at which point we locked eyes with them and held still, unblinking. Keep in mind that the distance between us was often no more than twenty or thirty feet! Eventually the elk would go on with their chewing and grazing, having seen us before and learned that we mean them no harm.

That's an example of what we call life in harmony with nature. A home surrounded by trees, flowers and animals; a land that's left to grow more or less as the Creator made it, wherein we as humans strive to damage as little as possible. More and more of the world's people are learning to reassess and perhaps sacrifice some of their wants and needs, making commitments to take less and appreciate more of the nature that still exists around them, wherever they live. Quite possibly this includes you.

Life in harmony with nature is best learned by doing, rather than by reading books like this, or by sitting around and thinking. In our home there are shelves full of volumes on nature subjects, yet we read them very little. There's wood to chop, water to haul, always something that needs doing or fixing, when we're not being distracted by the nearby paths and trails that tempt us to forget our daily chores.

Visitors sometimes wonder if our kids missed having conveniences like telephones, running water, or TV while growing up, but they really didn't have too much time to dwell on them, since all around us is a 24 hour nature channel, with the programs always changing. Once they got a little older their home schooling took up much of the day too, along with their chores, plus the gardens and animals whenever we had them. That's not to say they didn't yearn for things we didn't have, but I urged them to remember that in return for modern luxuries and entertainments, most kids don't have direct access to nature, a daily part of our life that I think they've always appreciated.

Another frequent question is, "Didn't your kids miss having a social life, contacts with other children, a knowledge of the bigger world?" What I tell them is, 'Hey it's pretty tough these days to be that much isolated.' Sure we've been out in nature the past 25 years or so, sometimes seeing little more than trees, mountains, stars and sky for weeks at a time. But in between we've also made trips to Vancouver Island, Disneyland, New York City, Toronto, even Europe, Cuba and Mexico. That's not to mention the countless pow-wow dances, tipi camps and tribal ceremonies we've attended at various places near and far. "But everybody can't just pack up and move out into the woods," others like to challenge. We eagerly agree, and hope that most people won't. There aren't enough woods left to hold us all. That's part of the problem. Bring the woods to you, wherever it is you've chosen to live. Even in downtown New York, I've seen green vegetable gardens growing on high rise balconies and down in ghetto vacant lots; newly planted trees and birdhouses; masses of people enjoying parks and seaside beaches. Just the way you shop and buy things, and the way you discard them afterwards, can bring you closer to a life in harmony with nature.

"I could never live like that!" is still another comment we hear from skeptics. 'Oh yes you can,' I'd like to tell them, 'if that's what you want to do.' Sometimes I'm tempted to add that, at the rate things are going in the world, we might all soon *have* to live without the conveniences and luxuries that most everyone now takes for granted. Our society certainly can't continue on its present course for much longer, though my kids call me a pessimist when I start talking like that....

Those of you who have already found your own home in nature will probably recognize many of the experiences you read on these pages, since you'll have gone through your own variations of them. For the rest of you, may these tales inspire good thoughts and perhaps encourage you to have even more love and respect for nature than ever before.

A family portrait back when the kids were still small.
From left to right: Okan, Star, Iniskim and Wolf,
with Beverly and I behind them.
Photo by Brian Clarkson

1.

Wilderness Renegades

Our old beloved dog Boss is dead and gone, no more to wag his tail eagerly in greeting when we come home from town, nor at the start of another hike down one of our many trails. I'll miss his loud panting in the heat of summertime, and the frozen whiskers on his face when its thirty below. I'll miss that look of love and dedication in his dark brown eyes. Today I put his blanket-wrapped body into a wooden box and nailed it shut, then hauled him by toboggan across our snow-covered field to the forest's edge, where a mound covers similar boxes containing our previous family dogs, including Boss' mom Tippy (most faithful and - at 15 - oldest of them all) and his neurotic sister Baby, who may have worried herself to an earlier death.

We're all in shock here at home, because unlike any of the others Boss didn't just get old and die, he was killed by a trio of wolves, and it happened right out in front of our house! A thin layer of fresh snow told the whole story: His defense of home; the bitter fight; then his suffering last journey back down to our old house - now empty because we built a new one - where he grew up and spent his best years with his sister and mom. We found him there the next day, frozen solid in the January cold, laying under his favorite tree, his old clouding eyes left open like frozen marbles, his shiny white teeth still bared. Twenty feet ahead of him tracks showed where his enemies stopped once more and gathered, before they moved away through the snow and left him to die.

So now I'm wondering what to do about my mixed emotions, having always loved wolves, but loving Boss even more. It's as though someone I've really respected has suddenly done me a serious wrong; like a friend who has stabbed me in the back, taken something precious away because the opportunity happened to present itself.

Wolves are special animals around our household. While growing up I never accepted the "big bad wolf" theory that is still common in many parts of our society today. To me these noble animals are an important part of the wilderness areas that still exist within North America; I've cheered whenever I heard they had come back to another of their old domains. This enthusiasm is furthered by having both my first and last name in common with them.

In the early 1970's, after we moved to this homestead, when our boys Iniskim, Okan and Wolf were just starting to grow up, we never saw wolves around here; some said they were gone forever, although our land is within the range of those who survive in such famous national parks as Banff, Waterton and Glacier. All we ever used to see around here were coyotes; big, thickly-furred ones that we came to know as bush wolves. They're always a pleasure to watch when they trot across our field, or when a pair of them stop to tumble and play. Yet their paws aren't half the size of a real wolf's, nor is their bravery and strength. They never caused us to worry about having the boys playing out alone in the woods.

Mind you, I did see the occasional tracks of a real wolf, usually in the woods near our home, maybe once every couple of years, after a fresh snowfall, apparently always made by a lone individual who seemed to be passing hurriedly through our area in the night. The prints were usually so big and impressive that I fairly ached with yearning to catch even just a brief glimpse of their makers.

The day finally came when such a one made an appearance around here, but wouldn't you know that I'd be off riding trains at the other end of the continent! Everyone else in the family was home, so at least I got to hear their excited accounts. The main thing was that this first wolf didn't just hustle through in the night, but instead came right up to our house in broad daylight. It must have been a lonely male, since there was a lot of tail wagging and attention paid by him to Tippy, who was then an eligible "single mom." It was early enough in the morning that our three boys were still in bed, so I'll let Beverly tell what she saw from the kitchen window after Tippy and her kids Boss and Baby started barking furiously.

"The front windows were all frosted up from the cold so I couldn't see a thing at first, until I held my warm hand on one of the panes and melted a looking space. Just then the dogs were running across the field towards the house at top speed, coming from the forested hillside beyond. When they got nearer I could see in the early morning light that something was chasing them. At first I thought it was another dog, then I realized it was a silver-coloured wolf, a real big one at that. It startled me so much that I yelled out to the boys, "Quick! A wolf is going to kill Tippy!

"The boys threw on their moccasins, jackets and hats, grabbed their rifles, then went rushing past me out the front door thinking our family dogs were about to be killed. But I was just noticing that the wolf was now bowing down on the ground near Tippy, its nose between its paws, wagging its tail and acting submissive, apparently wanting to be a friend. The dogs were barking ferociously, standing just outside of where I was." From here we'll let Okan take over the story:

"Mama was up before us kids, making breakfast on the stove. All of a sudden she was shouting, 'Quick, get your guns, a wolf's gonna eat our dogs!' Iniskim and I jumped up and grabbed our rifles. I was in the lead, jamming shells into my 30/30 while heading out the front door, though I now wish we would have stopped and looked outside first.

"The dogs were barking like crazy, and here was this great big silver wolf about twenty feet from us, looking at them. It ran a little ways when we showed up, but then it stopped and looked at the dogs again. We could have shot it easily then, but that's not the way we learned to act towards them. Our three dogs would chase the wolf when it ran, but as soon as it stopped the two younger ones, Boss and Baby, turned and ran back to the house; only their mom stayed. She and that wolf actually touched noses, smelling each other, while we stood there and watched. Tippy was growling the whole time, but the wolf was wagging his tail and obviously wanted to be friends.

"Tippy was doing her best to act mean, so we had to laugh when that wolf started jumping up and down, all around, sort of like an excited pup, not at all scared of the chubby old dog (she was then about ten). Tippy finally turned away and started trotting back to the house, so the wolf followed right behind her. It took her a few moments to realize it, then she spun around and tried to attack, but the wolf took off quicker. He ran just a little ways, then turned and started jumping around again, wagging his tail and obviously hoping Tippy would get the hint and also play. Instead, she took off after him again, so he made another short dash, then repeated his playful antics. Tippy wasn't in heat at this time, but her daughter Baby began hers right after, so he must have smelled that. After about three or four of those chases with Tippy, the wolf finally gave up and trotted away, and we never saw him again after that."

The next time we did see a wolf around here was on the morning of Beverly's fortieth birthday, and this time I was home too, working at the typewriter in my nearby caboose. Suddenly Okan came rushing up the steps, telling me with short bursts of breath, "Come quick with your camera - there's a wolf down by the house!" At first I leaned back in my chair and said with a smile, "Sure - April Fool!" Beverly's birthday is on April the first. But, knowing his looks the way parents know their kids, he soon had me convinced that this was no joke. "Alright," I finally told him, "but even if there *was* a wolf at the house when you left, it won't be there now, after the noisy bike ride you just made across the field."

Lo and behold, the "birthday wolf" was still standing within easy sight of the house, some two or three hundred yards distant. It was a big black one, facing our three dogs, who were only about twenty feet away, barking their heads off. His body looked husky and formidable, even more so with an unusual grizzled silver mane, yet he showed neither aggression nor fear, even when I took a few steps in his direction to get a clearer photo. He held his ground, looking my way, but ignoring the barking dogs completely. Finally he turned and trotted a few yards, then stopped to look back once more, before heading slowly and proudly into a thick stand of small pines. Our dogs ran up to the edge of these, sniffing excitedly along his trail, but they dared not follow him into the forested depths beyond.

Okan and I got to see this black wolf a second time, a couple of months later, when eldest daughter Monique came by for a visit during which we took her by canoe down a wild stretch of the Kootenay River. There he suddenly was, standing on a sandy bank overlooking the water, silently watching us approach. When we got too close he ran, disappearing over a nearby knoll, but after we got the canoe to shore and ran up that knoll ourselves he was standing still again, not far from us. Had we been hunters we could have shot him either time. I wanted to shout and tell him that, but instead the four of us just stood in silence, looking at each other, until he finally loped away, leaving only blurred, hand-sized prints where his feet briefly touched the sand.

Wolves can be hunted all year in our part of the Rockies, which means the few we've seen never lasted long. Some weeks after that second sighting of the silver-necked black one, a fellow in a nearby village shot him down, then had him mounted for display in his den, while we miss the sight of him alive and coming around.

Time went by, daughter Star grew up, and her brothers got their own vehicles. They had gone to work one day when this next wolf story got started, one that has since turned into the most complicated encounter of all. Tippy had died of old age by then, so only her kids Boss and Baby were at home with me. It was a quiet winter morning and I was again working at my caboose desk when the dogs started barking excitedly up at the old family house, about 200 yards away. The sound of their barking told me a stranger was approaching, so I grabbed my binoculars and saw right away that whoever might be coming had been preceded by a dog. A rather big dog at that, I noticed with dismay, having nailed up a sign at our parking lot requesting visitors to keep their pets on a leash. This one was loose, and at the moment he was standing about ten feet from the front door, against which the two dogs were now backed, keeping up their ferocious barking.

The visiting dog seemed to have on a collar - somebody's big husky, I thought at first, until I realized the animal was actually a big silver wolf. He was now halfway up on the porch, only four or five feet from the dogs, waving his tail eagerly. But the dogs weren't buying his offer of friendship, having spent too many years being challenged by various animals passing by. I again grabbed my camera and rushed out for a picture, but the moment he saw me he ran away, disappearing like a ghost even before reaching the forest shadows. I went up to check his prints in the snow and found them to be more than twice the size of those made by our dogs, who were border collies.

A couple of days later I was home alone again, working in my caboose, when the dogs started barking, so I rushed outside thinking of wolves but finding instead a smiling, bearded fellow coming towards me with a small portable television antenna in his hands.

I consider television to be the main cause for a lot of problems in the world, so I've never allowed one here at our place, although oldest son Wolf once tried to hide a little battery operated one under his bed. I thought maybe this time one of his younger brothers was trying to test that rule again, and had gotten a friend to come down with a helping hand. I was ready to send him and that antenna on their merry way when he asked, "Do you know that there's a wolf around here?"

I swore under my breath, thinking this guy was not only bringing parts for an unwanted television, but now he was also after my friendly wolf. Instead he introduced himself as Mel and said, "Listen here," then turned up a dial on a little electronic gizmo that suddenly began to emit loud beeping signals. "That's him, he's over there," he said knowingly, gesturing with the antenna in a direction that made the beeping grow louder. He wanted permission to pursue that signal through our land, telling me that he was a volunteer for a group studying wolf behaviour in our part of the Canadian Rockies. The silver wolf was part of that study, a young male who grew up with a pack in nearby Kootenay National Park, from which he had lately disappeared, possibly taking along a small female.

"At first nobody could figure out where he went," Mel explained, "but they were looking towards the east, around Crowsnest Pass, and on over into the Alberta foothills." It seems the last collared wolf to depart from Kootenay Park ended up getting shot by an old Alberta rancher, the kind who shoot wolves first and ask questions later.

Pulling on a pair of tall boots to protect my deerskin moccasins from the deep fresh snow, I eagerly joined the pursuit of that electronic beeping - a crazy sound to be coming from such a noble animal so deep in the wild river forest. Knowing the terrain well, I guessed that he was heading for the main river channel, Mel saying that the study group would be interested to know if the wolf went on across. The water around here is fast and cold, with broken sheets of ice often making it difficult to come ashore.

It was the big silver wolf without doubt, for his tracks were huge wherever we could see them clearly underneath the pines, though mostly there was just a wide swath in the deep snow to show where he'd passed. Mel happened to be driving along the highway that morning with his electronic locater turned on when he got strong signals from our direction, having used the same method a few days days earlier to first locate the missing wolf. The Kootenay River continues south from here into the state of Montana, so it was important to stay in touch with the wolf in order to see if that's where he'd go.

Moving quickly and silently through the white powder, the electronic signal grew ever louder to indicate that we were getting closer, when suddenly from another direction a second swath came through the snow and joined the first one. Under the next big tree we could plainly see a new set of footprints, mostly made right over the big ones, though in size a lot smaller than them.

"It's the female," Mel said with certainty, increasing his speed and now even more determined to catch sight of them. Suddenly, as we stepped out into a small open meadow, we got a quick glimpse of our quarry on the far side, just a flash of grey that immediately disappeared into the dense willow brush, less than a hundred yards away. Upon reaching that spot we saw a flat patch in the snow underneath a small pine tree, indicating that we'd disturbed their attempt to curl up for some rest, or perhaps for a snuggle. Apparently they had not been aware that we were so close behind. We were both thrilled by the sighting, and I silently promised to do all I could so this pair might roam in my area undisturbed, though I knew that would be a challenge once word of their presence got out to some of the local hunters.

The two wolves had immediately separated upon leaving their bed, freshly plowed snow showing the smaller one heading further down towards the river while the big one headed back uphill in the direction from where we had come. Having accomplished our main goal, we gave up the chase and followed an easier trail back out of the bush.

Mel surprised me along the way by saying that he'd once been quite a wolf hunter. "Killed several before deciding I'd had enough," he told me, "so now I'm trying to give something back instead." He said several volunteers spend their spare time with tracking antennas like his, trying to follow wolf movements in our part of the Rockies to find out how many there are, how far they range and - of special importance - what impact they have on other wildlife. Killing them all year round is partly justified by hunter claims that wolves kill a large number of deer and elk, so keeping track with the help of electronics would provide some actual facts, not just idle speculation.

After this big wolf had been around our area for a while with two females keeping him company, Mel reported finding fresh killed remains of deer and elk every two or three days along their trails, which is more than I had expected. He did add that these animals were mostly old, injured or sickly ones, and that the bloody trail stretched for some fifty miles up and down our valley, so that the killing was spread out and not concentrated on any one herd. Still, hearing that a dozen or more big game animals were being killed around here monthly by this trio of wolves helped raise the ire of sporting hunters and made it harder for those of us wanting to defend their presence. Hunters weren't saying much about the thousands of animals they shoot every fall, nor about the similar numbers being slaughtered along highways and railroad tracks. As in most emotional conflicts, the facts often have been and continue to be presented rather selectively.

The next summer came and went with only a few wolf sightings, although Mel found a den not far from our home in which one of the trio gave birth to some pups. The emotional issue heated up further when a noticeable decline was discovered in our region's elk herds, which was immediately blamed on "an increase in wolves" (along with cougars and bears), although this problem had been developing for some years and was, in my opinion, caused mainly by overhunting and by the destruction of habitat rather than by the natural thinning of predators.

The snows of this winter showed plainly that the wolf trio was still around. During my outings on foot and with cross-country skis I frequently came across their fresh tracks. So it was one day not long ago that Beverly and I were skiing along the edge of a small forest, when fresh wolf tracks suddenly crossed right in front of us. I stopped to study them, wondering if it was the trio, noting that the big prints were there. Then our two dogs located a deer, recently killed nearby and only partly eaten, the well chewed carcass half hidden in the snow by a big mound of deer hair that had been purposely scraped over it. It was the first fresh wolf kill I've ever seen, so I joined my dogs and checked the details with interest.

There was one big problem with this discovery, however. We were leaving early the next morning for a tribal ceremony across the mountains, where we'd be gone for a day and a night, leaving the dogs home alone. Now that they'd had a good taste of that fresh killed deer there would be no way to keep them from coming back later, after we were gone. The only alternative that I could see was to bring the remaining carcass home. If the wolves found them eating their kill out in the bush, the dogs wouldn't last long, nor was I sure that the big wolf would be friendly to them like he was before, if he and his friends were to encounter our dogs away from the house.

When my plan became known to Beverly and Star there was great outcry; they said I was tampering with nature, taking away the wolves' food. I countered that the wolves had killed this deer within my own territory, that I moved here first, and that by nature I had every right to claim what I had found. "Survival of the fittest," I reminded them, but they were still unhappy with my decision. The dogs were thrilled, of course, wagging their tails much of the way home as they followed me and my loaded toboggan. I figured the wolves would have far too much fear of humans to come near our house, even if they decided to track the meat that I took away with me. And incidentally, I did leave them some behind.

But then we came home from our trip and found that Boss had been killed in our absence - disemboweled while defending his own home. His young buddy Ernie was mighty glad to see us, staying hidden in the hay bales along side our house until we were almost at the door before daring to come out. A good-sized golden retriever, he had been partly disemboweled himself the previous fall, when barely a year old, though we thought at the time that he'd had a run-in with some big mama bear.

There was more hue and cry in the household over this calamity, and my disregard for their warnings, but tracks in the snow showed that the wolves hadn't followed their deer carcass down here at all, in fact they had not even gone back to look for it at the place where they left it.

Instead, by coincidence they'd run into a big, old cow elk grazing in deep snow beside one of their regular paths, where they came down from surrounding ridges to head for the river's shore, quite close to our house. I found the half-eaten elk in dense brush not far from our house, then followed the three sets of bloody tracks where they came up onto our field, past our house, on the way back up to one of those ridges. There was a full moon out so old Boss had seen the trio quite well, I'm sure, even with the cataracts that were slowly forming in his eyes. I imagine he went out in front of the house barking as he'd always done, letting them know they were in his occupied terrain.

Wolves coming from a fresh kill can be pretty feisty - especially when there's three of them and one is exceptionally big. In addition, I learned from later tracking that one of the females was in heat, so it may be that the big wolf not only considered Boss to be challenging their passing and threatening their hidden food, but that he was even a possible rival for his lady. Never mind that a vet in town eliminated that option for Boss years ago. Whatever the reason, the wolves made a quick charge during which Boss put up a valiant fight - leaving a small, circular multitude of tracks trampled into the snow - before one or the other of them got hold of his vitals with sharp teeth and tore him open. With that, twelve years of companionship for him and I suddenly came too an end. The consolation was that his old age ailments sometimes made him pretty feeble in recent times, especially on colder days and nights. So this way his suffering was cut short, and what's more, he died a warrior's death.

As sort of a footnote to this story, the big silver wolf was shot not too far from here shortly after this, along with one of his female companions who was wearing the ragged remains of a broken old radio collar. That she-wolf had been tagged in Alberta, then tracked down to Montana, back up to British Columbia, then down again to Montana and over into neighboring Idaho, before joining up with the much younger but larger silver wolf. Their tanned hides are probably still "hanging out" together, but now on somebody's wall. And if you're wondering why I didn't just shoot them after they killed my friend Boss, you'll have to ask the two ladies in my household, for it was they who strongly insisted that I should allow them to live. In fact, the trio came through here again the next night by moonlight, but I only fired my rifle into the air to let them know how I felt - and to discourage them from coming back to bother poor, lonely Ernie.

Rabbit and Wind

Today a white rabbit ran alongside me, like the wind;
I was driving my pickup truck;
The rabbit was running along like the wind.
Wind, blowing through life, with its breezes, its gusts, its many calm times.
The wind is my friend; my shadow; it echoes my laughter and muffles my crying. Sometimes it can make me cry.
Other times it sounds like it's crying.
The rabbit doesn't know any of this, or doesn't have time to think about it if he does know it.
The rabbit is running like the wind, for the sake of his life.
He thinks my truck and I are out to get him.
We are a thunderstorm, a hurricane.
Did he feel foolish after we passed out of sight without even showing him any recognition? Or did he just slow down with the settling dust and wiggle his ears?
All that is mere conjecture at this point.
I can only say with certainty that if Bre'r Fox had shown up, he'd have had an easy meal. Would that be blamed on the wind, on me, or on the naivety of the simple rabbit? Was the Creator chuckling while deciding that rabbits will sit dumbfounded often enough so that foxes (and others) can catch enough of them to keep themselves alive? It is from such simple thought processes that modern industrial systems were probably developed. But that's another story....

3.

A Homestead of Our Own

"Back to the Land" was the theme for a lot of us young people in the 1960's, and in the 1990's a new version of it seems to be growing in popularity. There are great differences between the two, mind you. The sixties crowd mostly rushed out of the cities with starry eyes and romantic notions, rather than with money, skills and planning, whereas nowadays many high-earning workers opt for country life so they can perform their jobs via computers, without the wear and tear of living in a crowded city. In some cases the new pioneers tried it the first time around too, but whereas then they simply wanted a place to pitch a tipi for "subsistence living," they now want quality life on land whose environmental status is of great concern.

Having myself lived successfully "out on the land" for over 25 years means that pretty well anybody could do so if they cared to, since I left the city with little money and even less in practical skills. I did walk away from a good teaching job, bringing a wife and two little kids who put their faith in my daydreams.

During the final years of city life I collected good used farming tools and other basic gear, plus leather for the craftwork skills I'd taught myself. I also cobbled together a little 32-page book that I called *Good Medicine: Life in Harmony with Nature,* which was sort of a rough blueprint for a possible future. It combined outdoor stories and poems with photos and articles about native life, meant to serve as inspiration for the kind of life I was setting out to learn.

From my Swiss father I inherited a love for mountains, although his was for the Alps and mine has been for the Rockies. For a thousand dollars down I was able to buy a 140-acre abandoned farm along the Columbia River, in the Canadian part of the Rockies, during an era when such land was still cheap, and when Canadian citizenship was freely offered to ambitious people who qualified in their desire to make a new life. Land prices have gone up a lot in the quarter century since then, but so have wages and immigration requirements.

The place we got had no home, so we spent the first season using a small tipi and our old VW bus for shelter. We got by all summer with only a Coleman camp stove for cooking and heating. By fall we had a more solid home, an 8'x12' insulated wooden shack sold to us by an old Swedish logger named Oscar, who figured he'd spent enough winters in the Canadian Rockies, so he used the $250 he got from us for a one way trip back to Sweden, where I heard he later died. He was among the first of many interesting outdoor people I've met since, and he was around long enough to cushion my initial impact to homestead living. Over the years he'd homesteaded and logged nearly every farm in our area, surviving alone outdoors one night in the cold of winter, pinned beneath a huge pine he'd cut so that it fell and accidentally broke his back. His harnessed work horses headed back home which eventually caused a friend to come looking, and that's what saved him.

The little shack was built after another of his calamities. It seems he had a bunch of his cronies over for drinks in his previous home, and eventually they all passed out. During the night it got cold, then someone woke up and found the fire out, so in order to hurry the reheating decided to pour what he thought was kerosene on the remaining coals. The stuff was deadly white gas, meant only for the lamp. They barely got out with their lives, and later they helped old Oscar build the little shack so he'd still have a home. Sadly, by then he was otherwise landless, having lost his last farm during a card game in town one night. The consolation for us was that he built the little cabin on skids so it could be towed elsewhere (in case he got one of the old farms back, like he always dreamed), so we were able to hire another old logger to pull it half a mile to our land with his truck.

That little shack came equipped with a cast iron cookstove, a 1940's model coated with white enamel, which Oscar assured us was enough to keep the place heated even in the coldest of nights (which got down to -30 C. or more). An old man with a hearty taste for beer and other drink, he probably had to get up a few times during the night anyway, so maybe he didn't mind regularly dropping small pieces of wood into this stove's limited firebox every two or three hours. But I still preferred to sleep through until morning, which meant waking up to an icy cold stove and a freezing room. Still, if we'd been without kids this little cabin would have been good enough for our first few seasons on the land. A judicious search of lumber yards and building supply stores for bargain priced materials could see a similar cabin, well insulated, built for under a thousand dollars even in this day and age. A great many poor people around the world would be thrilled to have such a home. We tried to keep that in mind whenever we were tempted to complain about wanting something bigger and better to live in right from the start.

The little cabin was later used for guests, after I got some help to build a bigger one. Neither place had phone, plumbing or electricity, nor did I want any. The design was also simple; just a big single room measuring 18 x 24, which we sectioned off into quarters using wooden railings to mark out a sleeping area for adults, another for the two little kids, a third for the kitchen and the last for a general living space. One very rewarding feature was the picture window looking out at our small meadow, which had a thick green forest not far beyond, with the Rocky Mountains looming grandly in the background.

We learned quickly that buying little sacks of food every week at the grocery store didn't work out well for us, so we found a place that sold basic stuff in bulk, which not only saved us money but also assured us of having a steady supply on hand. This became all the more vital after the old VW bus broke down and got traded to a neighbor for a winter supply of firewood. We had dug a big hole in the ground and framed it to serve as a root cellar, reached through a trap door in the living room floor. From a local farmer we bought boxes of juicy, sweet-smelling apples, plus potatoes, carrots and other storeable vegetables.

Oscar showed me a spot uphill from our new house where birch trees grew and the ground was always wet. "I'll bet there's a spring under there," he said, so we arranged for a fellow with a backhoe to come out and do some digging. Before he arrived, this old guy helped me build a wooden box shaped something like an outhouse. He also had me buy a length of flexible plastic pipe and all the necessary fittings to make a simple water system. Fresh, cold water began running from the backhoe shovel about the fourth or fifth time it went down for dirt. We had the backoe operator dig the hole deep enough to hold the wooden box, which began to show standing water in its bottom after just a few minutes. Then we had him dig a trench on the downhill side in which we layed the plastic pipe, beginning with one end inserted into a lined hole towards the bottom of that wooden box. As soon as this simple system was in place the machine began to backfill, covering everything up and tamping the dirt and rocks down to stay in place. Within half an hour water started trickling from the other end of the pipe, which was dangling in midair not far from our cabin. The whole affair cost me about a hundred dollars and provided us with cold running mountain water free of charge whenever we wanted.

4.

The Loose Moose and My Old 44/40

More than a few lessons about wilderness living came to me the hard way, including the shooting of big wild animals. It may sound easy when you read in a book or magazine about someone else doing this; thousands of different hunting ways have been described in hundreds of volumes. Yet there's no better teacher than a pissed-off bull moose, eyeballing you from a short charge away, while you try to recall the words of all those smart writers. In my case I suddenly remembered the advice of an old outdoorsman retired to the city, who told me, "Don't bother bringing that 44/40 with you to the mountains, it's a worthless kind of gun." I thought he was just trying to discourage me, but here I was down to two shells, one of them in the chamber ready to fire, the other five stuck somewhere in that moose and he didn't seem very pleased about it.

What I had looked forward to most after getting settled on the land was to hunt our own meat, especially after the locals assured me it was easy. Up until then the biggest thing I'd ever shot in my life was an orchard-raiding skunk with a .22 rifle. Now suddenly I'd be allowed to shoot one each of deer, elk and moose, and I figured to do so in that order.

But when I finally went out to hunt my first deer, this darned bull moose turned up instead, courting himself a moose cow, even though the meadow I'd driven to was supposed to be used mainly by deer at this time of year, with the moose said to still be up higher. It didn't take long to learn that you can make general observations about wild animals, but as soon as you try to give specifics one will come along and do the opposite.

It was a long drive to reach that meadow, 12 miles into the wilderness from our homestead over a rough old logging road. I was using the family VW bus, having made no plans to bring back a 500 pound moose. But when I spotted that bull I decided that *he,* in the hand, was worth *two* later on in the bush. So I aimed my 44/40 and fired; it was that simple.

Let me tell you about this gun before I go any further. I got it from an old bearded guy who always wore a nifty cowboy hat and worked at the gun shop in Knott's Berry Farm's Calico Ghost Town down in southern California. A real westerner, or so I thought, with plenty of good stories to "prove it." When he heard where I was going *and* that I didn't have a hunting gun, he offered to sell me his, which was "a good un," he said. With it he'd shot "many an elk, moose and grizzly" of which he often bragged. "It'll knock 'em over at 250 yards and kill 'em clean," he assured me. It seemed so simple, standing there beside him in that little false front shop, paying my final installment and taking that fine looking weapon into my hands. Smooth action, fine polished wooden stock, the stamped name of Winchester making me proud as I pumped the oiled lever action a few times and looked through the open sights at some pigeons sitting on the roof of the old Calico Saloon across the street. My very own 44/40; "the gun that won the west." It didn't occur to me that it looked mighty clean, with no scratches or nicks, not like one would have expected from all the forests and mountains this old furry-faced gent was supposed to have traversed in order to get everything he said he'd shot.

With the motor off, I'd let the bus drift towards the trail that was to lead me back to this particular meadow, where the deer were supposed to be. It was easy to recognize the spot from an old burned out bulldozer some logger had left behind. I made my way quietly and soon spotted movement in the brush. It's hard to imagine what this does to a first time hunter with a fully loaded gun in his hand.

Although I trembled with excitement and anticipation, I had no plan to aim and fire until I could see what was making that tall brush move. There happened to be a big dead tree lying just ahead of me, so I slowly dropped down and crawled up to it, laying my rifle so it would be easy to shoot, then waiting to see what would happen next. Until then all the big wild animals I'd ever seen were either on the run, or getting ready to do so. I'd never observed one while keeping myself unnoticed, so this was a new experience in itself.

Eventually patches of black began to show through the leaves, while my ears caught the sounds of rustling, crackling, and munching. For a while I thought maybe it was a bear, but then I heard the thudding of hooves, and after that a strange-looking head appeared, staring my way. It seemed so tall, I thought whatever it was must be up on higher ground. Then I saw what appeared to be the black kid-brother of a giraffe, a gangly creature with a long neck, an odd bell shaped protrusion hanging below its chin, a fair sized set of flat horns, plus the ugliest big nose this side of Jimmy Durante. The moose had one more conspicuous trait, shared with chicano hot rods of the late 50s, that being his noticeably lowered back end. Yet in spite of all that, when he stepped out fully into view he was one impressive son of a gun, massive and muscular, dark and silent, standing sideways to me, about 150 yards away.

Suddenly there was another loud crack just behind him, then the bushes moved again, although he didn't flinch or even turn to look. No wonder, since it turned out to be his missus, about as big as him even without the horns, and about equally ugly. My mouth was dry and my breath came in gasps as I called on the jury of my inexperience and asked it what to do. The answer left no doubt: It was the way of the hunter, to track down his quarry and conquer it. A proud bull protecting his woman was as noble an adversary as the beginning hunter could hope to find, even though the rifle in his hand hardly made it a fair test. Or did it?

The cow moved back into the bush and the bull turned to follow, so I had but a moment to reconsider the jury's verdict. "Fire!" it said, and I did. The bull flinched and stopped, but then he just stood there, not even bothering to look over at me. The booming shot enveloped everything and echoed back from everywhere, while I stared in a momentary trance. Then I pumped a second shell into the chamber and quickly fired again. The bull flinched and stood there some more, still refusing to acknowledge my presence, while the airwaves again thundered and rolled. A third shell went into the chamber and again I aimed as

I'd been told, behind the front leg and about a foot down from the back, though the weird shape made it hard to tell exactly where this would be on that huge carcass, especially with all the drama and excitement. On my third shot he spun around as if I'd slapped him, and he faced me squarely. Then slowly and deliberately he started trotting my way. Damn, that isn't how it went in the stories, nor did the old bearded fellow mention pumping this many shells into his conquests. Hurriedly I fired a fourth time, but he still didn't go down, though after flinching this time he stood still for a few moments and dropped his head. I didn't know yet that moose can be very aggressive and are considered nearly as dangerous as bears.

Not until my fifth shot did that bull moose finally stumble to his knees, though I went ahead and pumped another shell into the rifle's chamber just in case. Sure enough, he got back up and started running my way again, getting within thirty or forty yards before I fired and knocked him clear down. But he still kept kicking and struggling violently, making enough racket to be heard even over the fading gunshot echo, so I put in my last shell and hit him again just as he was partly back up on his feet. Seven bullets before he finally collapsed in a heap and died. Said Oscar to some mutual friends a few days later, after he'd heard about it, "Yah, he shot the Loose Moose, but it was the weight of all that lead that brought it down."

Either that, or the weight of my conscience, once that wild meadow returned to its original silence. Except for a slight breeze, there wasn't a sound to be heard; nothing at all from the cow moose, and my shots had scared all the birds away; even the squirrels had stopped their noisy chattering. But just a few steps from me lay the mighty beast, more imposing in death than he'd been alive, and I had killed him. That it took so many shots left me humbled, as did an overpowering presence, even while another part of me felt pride for having accomplished what my daydream said I must, providing food for my family. I laid my knife upon its chest and prayed, as an old hunter and friend named Louie Ninepipe had told me to do, then I sang a song of victory - a chant of sorts, made up on the spot - to let the world around me know what I had done. This gave me courage, especially as another feeling came over me, the realization that I was way out in the wilderness with this mighty animal's spirit, just me and it alone.

Have you ever tried to butcher a bull moose? A tough job even in the best of circumstances, but it sure beat me on this day. For a start, I had a nifty sheath knife of which I was pretty proud - bought at a gun show for a few dollars from a guy who bragged how it was an original trade knife. From the looks of it he was probably right, it seemed very old and authentic, though otherwise still in pretty good shape. But it wasn't made of quality steel at all, and had it been I was still too unskilled at sharpening to have taken advantage of it. In this case the combination left me with a useless tool, not improved by a blade whose nice looking shape turned out to be unbalanced, making it more difficult for butchering.

The lesson I learned was not to go out into the wilderness with anything less than an excellent knife!

That knife would absolutely not cut the moose's hide, no matter how much I sawed back and forth. To be honest with you, had it been sharp as a surgeon's scalpel I would have still been in trouble, because I'd never butchered a big animal before, and wasn't even sure where or how to start. It was suddenly obvious that a moose I couldn't even move around was going to be one heck of a thing to learn butchering from. Furthermore, this was a late afternoon hunt, with the sun already gone and daylight fading fast. The moose had a strong spirit; the closer it got to night the more I noticed it. Finally I accepted defeat, picked up my empty gun and dull knife, trudging back out to my VW bus and wishing I were carrying a hind quarter on my shoulders, instead.

Luckily, I had a good friend, an old timer named Ted, who owned a pickup truck. He didn't hesitate for a moment when he heard of my plight, picking up a couple of sharp knives after looking at mine, bringing along some rope and an old piece of clean canvas.

It took a couple hours of hard work that night, even with the two of us and our sharp knives (one-and-a-half of us would probably be closer to correct, with me playing city slicker turned forest butcher while trying to keep my rear end out of the truck's headlights). The eerie part was that we caught a glimpse of the cow when we first drove up, standing not far from the downed bull. I guess since I didn't butcher him or hang around there for long maybe she thought he was just playing possum; I've seen other strange behaviour by mates and families of animals that were killed. In this case we could hear her moving around in the bush not far away, making a semi circle back and forth, though in the dark night I couldn't see her nearly black coat. Somewhere around the time I was struggling with an armload of fresh hot guts she disappeared, though I was so sweaty, hot and dirty that I never noticed and I think Ted was by now enjoying giving me directions so much that he didn't care. At one point I had to crawl part way into that bloody carcass to cut loose the lungs and heart.

In the eerie glow of the headlights I could see two or three bullet holes through the rib cage, but compared to the animal's size they looked mighty puny. I eventually found all seven bullet holes and six of the bullets, only one having gone clear through. A couple hit bone and just came to an end there, rather than working to bring the animal down. Perhaps it was the last shot that severed the aorta, which is what Ted said had probably killed him.

Getting this bull gutted was only the first big challenge; after that we had to load him up. We manhandled him from the ground up onto the pickup bed, me thinking time and again that we weren't going to make it. Were I to do this over again I'd just take the extra time and quarter the carcass right there, but I guess Ted had put in enough years working late nights out in cold forests, back when his logging machines would break down regularly, that he wasn't going to do it again just to make that moose any lighter. At any rate, we got it aboard, drove down to my old barn, drug it in through the door, then managed to raise it up with a rope tied to a rafter.

My latest lesson was that to hunt wild animals for meat, either know what you're doing or bring someone who does.

Ted ended up hauling a good part of that moose to his own house, where he had a big freezer that was nearly empty. He and his wife cut most of the meat into smaller pieces and wrapped it, then all of us (four adults and two kids) ate from it into the next summer. I never did end up shooting anything else that year, neither deer nor elk; reality had tempered my enthusiasm to be a constant hunter.

One reason this single wild animal lasted us so long is that we were also raising rabbits and eating them, though we had no experience with that either, at least not when we bought our first couple of does and a buck from an old farmer, having found some good homemade cages in our barn. Once these three got their act together, we were eating rabbit meat pretty steadily. It worked out good for a household without refrigerator, since we could eat up one animal before it spoiled. After that we bought a couple of ducks and some chickens, having still more empty cages available, though I told myself I should be building a good barnyard first. Since it was warm weather by then, I put the cages outside, up on blocks, not thinking that this was similar to sitting down by the bridge and dangling a long red worm in the water.

There were lots of wild animals in that region who would have enjoyed taking advantage of this greenhorn's naive offering of banquet ingredients - but a pack of local dogs got there first, and by the time I got up from bed, dressed and outside with a flashlight, most of the new menagerie lay dead or dying. I would have shot the dogs, but they ran off as soon as I came out the door.

Ironically, they belonged to one of our new hippie neighbors, a vegetarian family who had been chiding my ruthless murder of the moose and our barbaric eating of it afterwards. They tried to say that if we hadn't been raising the rabbits and ducks, their dogs wouldn't have gotten themselves into trouble. But as a carnivore I put on the more ferocious show - even though they had me outnumbered - so they ended up apologizing and shelling out twenty bucks to buy replacements. We kept the new brood inside of tight enclosures and had no more problems with dogs.

Now horses, they were a different thing for me. I fulfilled one of my childhood daydreams by putting up a tipi the day after we

got moved to the land - though it rained so much and the mosquitoes were so bad that we slept mostly in the bus. But for another of my dreams I needed a horse, preferably one I could also
work with, but mainly one to ride. And it had to be a pretty one;
I mean, who would daydream of something less? So I bought a
black and white pinto mare from the son of an old Swiss farmer
up the valley. This fellow seemed kind of strange, but he had a
nice little herd of horses and gave me a good price on the mare,
so I located someone who would haul her down for me and the
deal was made. I should have been a bit more leery after I saw
him smack her on the neck with a two by four when she balked
at getting into the borrowed trailer - a strange place as far as she
was concerned. But he said that was the best way to show a stubborn horse who's the boss, so I thanked him for the advice, said I
was naming her Matso-aki (meaning Good Looking Woman in
Blackfoot), returned his final wave and took her home.

I'd rented horses from stables now and then while growing up,
usually just for an hour or two, mostly plodding with them over
established trails. But I'd never received instructions for riding or
handling horses, even less for actually living around them. My
only other experiences with horses took place back in the old
country after the war, where teams of them still hauled lumber,
beer and other freight. These were *big* horses, unfriendly and
unapproachable to a small boy. Two incidents from that time
stand out in my dim memories. First, the very aged father of our
landlord was run down right before my eyes by a six-span team
and its loaded wagon, racing out of control on a snow covered
street. I thought he was dead and rushed home crying, but he
managed to survive and live a few more seasons, though his body
was so crushed that he could hardly move. During another winter
I was coming home from school, walking downhill on a narrow
sidewalk next to a small cobbled road, which curved at the bottom and followed the bank of a river. A team and wagon happened to start downhill just as I got near this curve, and soon the
driver was shouting for me to get out of the way, that he couldn't
stop. It was already icy that day, but suddenly I froze with fear as
well. Those horses seemed like deadly dragons, as they sort of

slid towards me, their nostrils steaming in the cold. I can still hear the frantic beat their hooves made while trying to regain traction, the jingling of reins and harness, the shouting of the driver standing up from his seat. Somehow they missed me, sideswiping the concrete wall just beyond. They managed to keep right on going as well, though never completely out of my life. Memories of them come back whenever I'm around horses, though these days it's no longer a problem. But it was when I first faced the stubborn and pretty Matsoaki, with just the two of us alone out in the wilds.

How many times she bucked me off I couldn't say, nor how often she broke her hobbles and tie down ropes to run away. Before winter I got her some hay and built a small corral, but eventually she took off again, this time during a ferocious snowstorm, so that I couldn't figure out for some time where she'd gone. It took numerous snowshoe trips through dense brush, forests and along the many frozen river channels to locate her trail. When I fianlly found her she was standing in a dense grove of slim aspens and birch, "penned" by deep snow into an area not much bigger than the corral, just barely surviving on the bark and twigs of surrounding trees. In places on her body she was already missing patches of hair, the start of an outbreak of mange, her overall appearance pitiful for her otherwise proud disposition and name.

Misery or no misery, that darned stubborn horse refused for the longest time to come back home with me through the deep snow. I had broken somewhat of a trail with my snowshoes on the way in and figured to make it better going back, but that still left her in snow way above her knees each time her feet broke through the icy crust, which was about every other step. I sure felt pity for that animal, plus annoyance with myself for rushing out to buy her in the first place.

At this point there was nothing I could do but coax, command and cajole, in all my best somewhat-afraid-of-horses kind of voice, pulling so hard on the rope around her neck that I frequently broke through the snow myself. It sure was no fun to try holding her while at the same time pulling the errant snowshoe back up. At one point during our slow progress she just keeled over onto her side, laying with her tongue hanging out, the deep snow still keeping her halfway upright. Exasperated, I did the same, at least until a big crow landed overhead and started squawking. Suddenly I felt as if I were looking down through that black bird's eyes, seeing the two of us seemingly dead, which spooked me into jumping up so fast that even the horse bounded upright, ready to try the tough trail again.

This story has a good ending, though it could easily have been a horse tragedy. Lots of hay and grain soon put weight back on her body, while to cure the spreading mange I followed Ted's recipe of applying liberal quantities of used motor oil that he'd drained out of his bulldozer the previous summer. Sure, the horse looked awful for a while, but the hair soon grew in thick and then she got back her good looks as well. Strange to say, she never made any further attempts at running away either!

Moving a family from the convenience of city life to the more rugged environs of wild country entails certain risks, not the least of them being a continuous testing of strength and will between married partners. In that way my first effort of going "back to the land" turned out less than successful, since our family split up and the property got sold (strangely enough to another "back to the land" couple who then also split up).

A few seasons later I tried it again with Beverly, and we're still at it more than 25 years later, having raised and home schooled four children, learned to build our own houses, developed a mail order business, and had more experiences with nature than I could have ever daydreamed in my young days. Our home is so far out that there aren't any near neighbors, though a rough three mile drive gets us to a good highway, and an hour has us "in town." There's no phone, television or electricity here, and if you want to get a vague idea of what that's like, just shut all yours off for a day and night and see how much different your life is.

Our dream was to build a nice log house, but so far that still hasn't happened. When we got here there was already a small 18' x 24' shack - albeit without insulation, interior walls, or even roofing paper - but it was immediately available and needed only minimal work, whereas the log house would have required time, money and skills that were all in very short supply.

To improve that shack I began by covering it with rolled roofing to keep out the rain, then I insulated the walls and covered them with cedar boards that a local lumber mill let me have for $5 a truckload because they were "third grade," though they've now been here for over 20 years and are still holding up just fine. Income was pretty sparse from what had turned into a little series of books, so we scavenged some of the building material. For instance, most of the insulation for walls and ceiling came from an old abandoned shack up the valley, though the two-inch fiberglass stuff was way too thin by today's standards. For comparison, our new studio home has 10 to 15 inches of insulation everywhere, plus a complete plastic vapour barrier which I didn't even think of including when we fixed up that old cabin.

The first addition we made was a porch out front for storing jackets and boots and for getting out of the wind. This also helped to warm up that part of the poorly insulated cabin quite a bit. One priority was for me to have a quiet place to write, something I'd have to do steadily to pay the bills. Thus, I added another room to the north side, which became our home's coldest section, though it sure made the rest of the place a lot warmer. We had three wood-burning stoves in the house at this time, one in each room, though none of them was worth a darn on hindsight. For the kitchen we used an antique Monarch cook stove passed on from my adopted grandma, which worked fine as long as someone was nearby to feed it wood. The other two stoves were both sold as so-called "airtights" which they definitely were not. Of these two, the fancier one was a cast iron box heater, the other an economically-priced oblong tin can, taking wood through a round lid at the top, a popular beginner's stove noted for its tendency to get red hot and fry everyone out of a room when you're visiting, then for turning into an icy cold box during the middle of the night. All three stoves were hooked to ordinary sections of stovepipe that went up through our cedar ceiling and pine roof with the barest of protection. We're darned lucky we never burned the place down, since in those days we had neither wells nor any other handy source of water nearby, nor had we been able to afford the fire extinguishers that we keep on hand nowadays. *For safety's sake, if you're thinking of switching to wood heating, be sure to get experienced help and first class equipment. Get the best stove your money can buy, and don't hook it up until you've built a sturdy chimney. After all these years we wouldn't have our home without one.*

That add-on writing room on the cold north side also doubled as our bedroom, and boy was it chilly at times! Drafts everywhere from the cheap materials, amateur workmanship, and the lack of plastic vapor barrier. That room's main flaw was that I built it so as to fit under the existing roof of the cabin, which gave it a very low sloping ceiling and a floor lower than the main room, uninsulated and always cold. We were young and tough then, so when it got too bad we just threw another blanket or two on our bed and checked to make sure the kids were warm. Now that arthritis nibbles at me (along with other signs of old age) I wonder how much those tough nights might have contributed? Guess I'll never know, but for myself at least I get a lot of satisfaction from the memories of our "pioneering."

We learned from that mistake and made the next add-on room to the old cabin a great deal better. It became the "kids' room," another 6' x 12' box with sloped ceiling, like the one we used for writing and sleeping, but this time with a floor *higher* than the main room - to catch the warmth headed up. Also, with a sheet of plastic under the inside panelling, which kept out the worst of the winds. What's more, I built a sleeping platform down the whole length of this room, another couple of feet higher yet, so where the kids had their mattresses and pillows it was always the warmest in the whole house.

This kids' room became a necessity when our third son Iniskim was born during our second year here. Three little boys required a room of their own, even if only a compact one like this. We added a full length step alongside the sleeping platform, whereupon the boys could sit and read, roll their toy cars, or land during the night if they rolled out of bed. Thus having three layers of floor space made that tiny room seem bigger and more practical.

The day Iniskim got old enough to be moved out of his crib and into an open bed in this room, joining his two older brothers, must have seemed like an important event to him, though he was not even two years old yet. At bedtimes he'd gotten into the habit of climbing over his crib bars to get a toy, or else to harass one of his brothers. When this happened, they usually told him to go back to bed, then if he didn't they'd eventually call out to us, "Ghee's up!" When Iniskim was first born, Okan could only pronounce his name as Ghee, which stuck as a nickname for a while. Upon hearing "Ghee's up," we'd either have to call from our room and tell him to get back to bed, or threaten to come in after him, which he seemed to take as an additional challenge.

On that first evening in his new open bed, I noted in my journal that I quietly walked in to find him laying there proudly, arms crossed under his head on the pillow, both legs propped straight up on a peeled pole that helped hold up the ceiling, singing not too quietly but apparently just to himself in a pleasant voice, "Ghee's up!....Mama, Ghee's up!" Over and over he repeated it, like a mantra, perhaps in celebration that the crib and its bars were gone at last, and that now he could actually get up.

5.

Trails of the Hunter

Hunting was supposed to provide some of our main food supply, yet four months after we first got settled on this homestead, I still hadn't been able to shoot anything and hunting season was about over. I had spent so much time and energy out on the trails with my rifle that I began to wonder if this was going to be a worthwhile pursuit. There were elk and deer tracks every day, yet I seldom saw any of the animals, and when I did they usually saw me first and took off. It was as if they knew the purpose of that rifle in my hand, for later that winter they frequently let me get quite close without running away, but I was then always un-armed. Maybe I was by then also getting a little more experienced at locating where animals were and how to see them.

We left for town early one Friday morning of the hunting season's last weekend, a heavy overnight snowfall having urged me to go buy some more food and supplies, in case we got stuck here for a long time without being able to drive in or out. It was to be the first winter for both of us to try living without neighbors or a public road.

The town trip went quickly, so that by mid afternoon we were already back home. After helping Beverly get the kids downhill to our cabin, I went back up twice more to haul food supplies down from the truck, using a heavy wooden toboggan I'd bought for five bucks at a second hand store. By this time the snow was nearly a foot deep and still falling.

Having already worked up a small sweat from the hauling work, I decided to stay outside and go for another hunt. I figured the fresh white carpet would let me see what had recently passed by and perhaps even to follow it. Sure enough, the parking lot and my truck were still in sight when I came upon recent signs that showed where two deer had run off, probably when we arrived. The trail headed uphill through a forest of pine, in the direction I most liked to walk, since it led to open hillsides with distant and dramatic views.

By the time I reached the first of these open areas I started getting tired, having slogged up and down through deep wet snow for well over an hour without let up, starting with the loads I brought from the truck. I stopped underneath a huge old yellow pine and leaned on its massive trunk for a rest. About that time I realized that what I had taken to be several boulders not far ahead were actually a bunch of grazing elk and they hadn't noticed me, or so I thought.

It was a herd of cows and calves, which was good since I had a cow tag. Ideally, it might have been more proper for me to seek out a big-antlered bull, but all I wanted at that point was meat for my family; the cabin walls had little enough room for our stuff, without needing the macho notion of large horns to hang up.

When I raised my rifle and turned my body so that I could take better aim, a young cow came charging out from behind a couple of trees quite near me, where I hadn't even noticed her presence. She must have been watching for me to make this wrong move; her alarm immediately got the rest of the herd on the run. Although the temptation to shoot was great, I managed to recall somebody's experienced advice to wait until an elk stops, which it generally will after a bit, rather than risk a wounding shot on the run. Sure enough, about 250 yards from me they all stopped, part way up a very steep slope, their heads turned to look back. Only the one cow had seen me, while the rest seemed unsure as to what the trouble was. She finally went on ahead some distance while the others continued to stand and look.

At the back of the herd and closest to me stood the biggest cow of them all. That she was in back because she was older and slower than the rest didn't occur to me. All I knew was that a big bunch of meat stood sideways within range of my gun. I aimed carefully below her shoulder and fired, but saw right away where the bullet sprayed snow and hit the ground several feet short of its mark. So I pumped in a second shell and fired again, though still nothing happened except for a tremendous noise, sounding all the worse because it instantly echoed from the cliffs towering above us. In fact, the noise was so awesome and wide ranging that the elk seemed uncertain as to its source, having still not seen me nor caught my scent, thus they didn't move.

It wasn't until the fifth shot that I made contact, with the big cow going down instantly, though still kicking her legs as if trying to run. She had been standing on a steeper slope than I realized, a fact that became apparent as I tried to climb towards her through the deep sloshy snow. She was still alive when I reached her, though the shot had broken her back. Unfortunately; she was hung up on a little rocky outcropping partway up that slippery slope, her body draped around a small poplar tree like a wet blanket on a clothesline. Having left my rifle down the hill for the climb, I was forced to use my skinning knife to cut her throat and end her struggle. But then my own struggle was ready to begin.

For a start, it took a lot of effort just to keep myself from slipping and tumbling down that slope, yet I was faced with an animal more than three or four times my own weight. Just to move that elk wasn't so hard, but I had to move it enough so that one half or the other would go up and around the slim trunk of that little tree. I ended up sitting down in the snow on the uphill side, resting a part of my weight on my feet, which were firmly up against the two sides of the elk's back. I began a slow rocking motion, each time pushing one side or the other a little harder, until at last the momentum caused the front end to go so far that the back end followed it over, and I nearly did too, digging my gloved hands as far into the rocky soil underneath the snow as I could, while trying to avoid getting a flailing elk hoof in my face, or taking off downhill after the sliding carcass.

What goes up must come down, and so it is with a dead elk and a beginning hunter who find themselves in rough terrain. She came to rest in a small level place, next to a little pine tree. That's where I gave my prayer of thanks, then stood back to take a look at what I'd done. As with my moose a couple of years earlier, I felt both thrilled at the prospect of many good family meals and humbled almost to the point of remorse for having ended the life of this noble creature. I still hadn't realized that by killing the biggest and oldest cow in the herd, I'd also opted for the toughest bunch of meat. Luckily, we had planned to dry much of it, and in that form the toughness is not so noticeable as it is when fresh. We did try cooking one or two steaks from this first elk before we admitted that she was best for drying, or stewing along with contents from our sacks of potatoes and carrots.

But there was a big problem for me between the time of shooting and the making of those stews, namely that the fresh killed elk lay at my feet some two miles away from the cabin, with a rough hilly trail through heavy unplowed snow, *and* it was just before dark. Furthermore, the sky was clear and the night was promising to turn quite cold. So I worked as quickly as my inexperienced hands and arms would allow, cutting open this big animal to take out its innards before the carcass should freeze too solid. Any elk hunter will tell you that it's quite a chore to gut a mature animal, all the more so when a beginner is doing it by himself in a rush by twilight. I managed to get all the main parts out in one big pile without cutting any of it open so it could spill and make a worse mess, although I was covered with blood and guts from head to toe and probably came closest that time to looking like my namesake. With my scarf tied to a branch to help keep away rival scavengers, I left the carcass behind and went home for the night with my rifle, not knowing just how bloody I looked until I saw Beverly's reaction to me in the lamplight. She still recalls it as one of the more frightening moments in our years here.

Wolf was four years old at this time so I wanted him to come along with Beverly and me the next morning to see how I had gotten our meat. I wanted her help with the butchering, especially since I would now be working with a frozen carcass. Okan was only a few months old, so there was no use trying to bring him. Instead, we waited to leave until he fell asleep for his morning nap, figuring to be back before his usual two hours was up. I gathered ropes, knives and an axe, along with two toboggans, on one of which I strapped a wooden box with a blanket inside for Wolf to ride in. The snow was too deep for a little guy like him to try keeping up with us on foot.

Having never butchered a frozen animal before, I had no idea
what amount of hard work lay ahead of us. Alternately cutting,
hacking and chopping, I slowly quartered the elk while my
hands remained in a constant state of nearly frozen, the only
thing preventing that being our constant movement. Unfortunately, the same wasn't true for Wolf, who sat still in his blanket
box and got quite cold, eventually crying and adding to our
woes.

At long last we were ready to take the first load home. Beverly
agreed to haul Wolf and one of the elk's front quarters. On my
own toboggan I took the other front quarter, along with both sets
of ribs and the complete "back strap," from which we get our favorite cuts of meat. My job was also to lead and make the trail
better, though it was rough going with the wet heavy snow and
awkward load. By the time we finally got home we found Okan
awake, standing in his crib, crying so hard that his voice was
hoarse and his eyes nearly swollen. We felt awful and never made
that mistake again with any of our kids.

Heading back up later by myself, I figured to make two more
round trips for the remaining meat. But by then it was sunny and
mild, with the snow melting faster and making the trip even harder. I was afraid that if too much snow melted I'd have to carry the
meat on my back, so I got stubborn and loaded both hind quarters *and* the big frozen hide for one single trip. It certainly wasn't
the easy way out of a predicament; I collapsed in a heap when I
finally got home, and didn't get up again for a while. Besides being heavy in the wet snow, the hind quarters stayed on that toboggan about as well as a scoop of fresh jello stays on a fork.
When they weren't slipping through the tie-down ropes, those
frozen pieces of raw meat would either hang up on trees and
bushes that we passed, else they would cause the whole load to
turn over. It was an experience and a lesson with a lot of suffering, that's for sure.

Beverly's ordeal with this elk wasn't over yet, for in keeping
with traditions passed down to us it was my job to do the hunting
and packing, but hers to cut up the meat and prepare it for use.
With most of it to be dried, she had to cut big chunks into thin

sheets and slices from morning till night for the next couple of days, until her hands were so tired that she could barely hold on to the knife. But we both got a lot of satisfaction for months afterwards, first seeing all that meat drying on strings across our cabin ceiling, then using it for meals until the next autumn's hunting season to keep our bodies strong for the wilderness living.

My kids laughed when I read them this story and said I should be ashamed to admit to such poor hunting. Well, I don't present it here with pride, but with the hope that my mistakes will alert some other beginners. I learned very quickly, there being no one to back me up when I made mistakes except for Beverly and a house full of little kids. Even so, there were other lessons yet to be learned from hunting and homesteading in this modern age. I won't burden you with a list of them, nor with a rundown of the elk and deer we've brought home since.

Having elk living on our land has given us many opportunities to watch them closely with binoculars and study their behavior. For instance, the first time we saw a big herd with a bull, we were surprised to discover that the cows communicate with each other through squealing. Of the nearly 20 cows in that herd, at least four took part in the "conversation," assuming that's what it was. It reminded me of sounds I've heard on recordings of whales.

Shortly after that first squealing session we also got to see a sparring match between two of the biggest cows. They suddenly turned towards each other, reared up on their hind legs, snorted once or twice, then commenced pawing the air until they ended up pounding each other with their front hooves. It wasn't a bloody battle, but the punches were serious and solid; I could clearly feel their reverberations 100 yards away, across the frozen ground. When they dropped back down to all fours, the hair on their backs stood straight up. They remained still for several moments, looking quite dazed, after which they just went on with their grazing. Most of the herd had stopped to watch this brief duel, but not the big-antlered bull, who was probably too concerned about battles of his own.

Beverly has developed an interesting relationship with deer

and elk over the years, mainly by whistling to them, "so they'll know who I am," she says. After initially running away when they first see her, as they usually do with people, they invariably stop when she whistles, then stand and watch her until she goes back inside a building.

Old timers claim there were no elk in this valley when settlers first came here in the early 1900's. That may be so, though the Kootenay Indians had plenty of traditional uses for elk hide and other parts of these animals, so they must have known them well. It could also be that elk were around, then disappeared for a time, as they've done occasionally since we've lived here, especially in the first years and now lately again.

That there weren't many elk on our land when we bought it was to be expected, since the previous owner had allowed an old salty outfitter to fence in his packhorses for year round grazing. In just a few seasons these big-footed blokes had chewed practically every edible plant down to the ground, or trampled it, so there was little reason for elk to come around. Even deer weren't much seen, though their main browse is brush, which the horses ate less of, yet they also stomped through it and broke it down.

Once we got rid of the horses it took about two or three years for the natural grasses to grow back thick enough that herds of elk began to depend on it again for their winter feed. About this time our only neighbor fenced his land and allowed a big ranch to run their cattle on it during the summer, making our ungrazed portion even more valuable to the wildlife. I say neighbor, although his home was 100 miles away and no one lived on his 7,000 acres of mostly forested land, which joined ours at one end. The only problem with the cattle was that the rancher who brought them didn't put up fences where our lands met, so the beasts eventually came down here, since we have the easiest water access. Initially, I was quite put out about this and ready to take legal action, then I learned that we live in a region that still has "open range laws," where *I* have to fence them out if I don't want them. Instead of doing that, I trained our dogs to chase the cows anytime they got near, often running along with them myself, rocks clutched in my hands, yelling at the top of my lungs. The experiences helped me to dislike cows even more than I already did. Beverly grew up in ranching country and figures, "most cowboys have this attitude that their cows are more valuable than elk and other wildlife." Deep inside she's still smarting from an earlier generation of "cowboys" who wiped out the buffalo herds her ancestors depended on.

Three or four other ranchers tried to use the neighbor's land for summer grazing, but each time their cattle would eventually get tired of our meadow and head further down into the riverside forests and channels, presenting a nightmare for the cowboys who were sent out to bring those cows in before winter. Never once did such a crew find all their wandering cattle, with the loss of just a couple head virtually wiping out the profits. I had nothing to do with the disappearances, though it must have seemed quite suspicious one year when a cow dropped dead right alongside our road, about a mile towards the highway. Luckily, the neighbors found it first, recognizing from its bloat that it had eaten too much fresh spring grass, so I made sure to mention that to any other ranchers considering this area for their cows. Word must have finally gotten around, after which no more cows were brought here, and that's when the elk population grew to its greatest. We also had several mild winters in a row, so there was a lot of good grazing even in amongst the trees of the forest. Bulls started fighting over herds of cows right by our house, their bugling and bellowing echoing back and forth across our meadow anytime of the day or night. This was a thrilling time for us, since normally mating and fighting by elk is mostly done high up in the mountains.

One autumn we had a very memorable ceremony here at home, attended by several of our closest friends, among them Joe Crowshoe and Mike Swims Under, two of the last elders familiar with certain tribal rituals that our group was then learning. Among the main animals honored in that ceremony was the elk, for whom we sang a song, sort of a chant, with the words, "Elk says, where I walk is holy." Simple words, but with deep meanings in their ceremonial context. We also sang for beavers, otters, eagles, crows, buffalo, deer, and many more. There happened to be beavers actually working on a new house and dam for themselves just a few hundred feet from where we sang and danced. The next morning, our youngest son Iniskim shot a big bull elk down the meadow from our house, providing us with winter meat, and the visitors with a taste of something special to take back home. This bull had been injured earlier in a fight, leaving him badly limping but still trying to guard his herd of cows. By tradition, he was needed for food so we were allowed to shoot him; otherwise the birds and animals represented in our ceremony are not allowed to be killed by the participants.

This made me wonder how many peoples of the world once knew and practiced rituals or other forms of honor and respect to birds and animals; I'd guess most of them, if not all, at some point in their history. Strange to say, if we interpret this kind of devotion fairly liberally we can say it continues even in these modern times with such songs as "The Lion Sleeps Tonight," "Rockin Robin," or even "The Woody Woodpecker Song." All of them are tunes giving recognition to something in nature.

For a few years there were a lot of elk around, then the numbers started declining again, although the Fish & Wildlife people seemed to be doing all they could to make aerial counts and set hunting quotas accordingly. We did notice during those few autumns when we had bull elk right down here during hunting season that within a short time they were gone. Shooting them should have been closed, because in the weeks after that the herds of cows all showed up alone, then the following spring only a few of them had calves. The bulls were shot too soon for the mating needs of the herds. Now, for the last couple of years, we've hardly seen any bulls down here during hunting season nor many of them afterwards, leading us to assume there is more hunting going on in our whole region than the animal populations can bear. Part of the season is also open for cows and calves, making things even worse.

When we had lots of elk around, they would at times disappear practically overnight, staying gone for days, even weeks. After finding fresh tracks all over our meadow day after day, it's always strange to go out and suddenly see no more signs, as if the elk had all gone for a trip to the warmer south or someplace. Usually there's a weather change to go with this disappearance, especially if the field is covered with soft snow when it warms up, then we get a cold snap that turns it all into a sheet of ice. Of course, when there's a storm blowing across the land the elk usually stay off the meadow till it's over, but afterwards they get right back out and start pawing through the snow for food. Hunting season usually closes around the end of October or sometime in November. The longer it is afterwards, the less spooked elk will be when they see us. Since we live right out on our meadow, we get seen by them a lot, even though we try not to be disturbing about it. They tolerate us much more at night than in the daytime, but whenever it is they usually stop grazing and stand still to watch, letting us get within 100 yards or so, as long as we don't move directly towards them, don't talk loud or make other sharp noises. If we meet those basic concerns of theirs, most elk will soon get back to eating. In the daytime they won't let us get half that close, and if they get spooked they usually head right for the woods and leave the clearing altogether.

One of the startling thrills I experience regularly when I go out walking around here is to hear a sudden, loud bark, sometimes followed by a deep growl, as if coming from the throat of a 500 pound German Shepherd. This is the warning sound of an elk saying "I know someone's in my territory and I'm getting mad about it, but I don't know who it is or whether I might actually run if I see them." Cows with calves are especially likely to bark, but any of them will do it.

One summer a big ranch from up the valley ran about a hundred head of cattle on our neighbor's land, though like all the rest, they lost money on the deal. By the end of summer when they rounded up their animals, four or five turned out to be missing.

This outfit might not have had that problem if they'd come through on a promise they made to me in the Spring, when they first brought the cows here. At that time there was still a fence between our land and the neighbor's, though a lot of it was hanging on the ground and some of the posts were rotting. The ranch foreman said if I was to unhook *all* the wire, his men would come by and plant new posts, then tighten the fence and nail the wire back up. I fulfilled my part, but for the rest of the year all that wire just remained laying there, until I finally rolled it up and hauled it to the dump the next year. So I was naturally not very happy with this outfit by the end of summer, their cattle having chewed up a great deal of our field and crapped all over it. I'm used to the much neater droppings of elk, who may eat much of our field also, but don't leave anywhere near the same signs of dust, digestion and devastation.

One day I heard the dogs barking as I was quietly writing, so I looked out to see four horseback riders going casually across our field, though not headed in our direction. I chased after them on foot and called for them to stop, demanding to know why they were riding through my "yard" as though it was their own. The foreman, an unpleasant, old time, cowboy type, said defiantly that they were out "looking around for their missing cows." I informed him that he could darned well do his looking somewhere else rather than on my private property, that it was bad enough having to put up with the cattle all summer. He in turn said that those missing cows were worth $1,200 each and that he was "darned well going to look for them." Riding with him were two young guys and a strange looking lady in movie type cowgirl gear. When I suggested the R.C.M.P., he grinned and said gleefully, "They won't do anything - you have no fences up, nor are there any keep out signs." That's apparently the way fellows like him operate in the outdoors. He excused their failure to do the promised fencing by saying, "We had no time or money, since we're already losing plenty on these cows anyways." So I said, "If you're losing so much money, why don't you just shoot them and raise rabbits instead?" That's what I was doing, and they were pretty easy to take care of. They finally rode away and I'm glad to say that they've never returned.

6.
That Damned Barbed Wire!

Through the years here I've probably gathered twenty pickup truck loads of "junk" left from the past 100 years when "white men" first began to settle in this valley. Much of that load was rusty barbed wire, strung seemingly everywhere, often from tree to tree. During countless punctures and scrapes that I've received from my *un*fencing work I've had occasion to defame whoever it was that invented barbed wire, hoping he strangled on the stuff himself, especially when I found chunks of elk skin or deer meat dried to some of the barbs along with numerous thick clumps of ripped out hair. I've found barbs with bird feathers, others with the soft furs of such night-walkers as wolves, bears, coyotes, and beavers. It makes me wonder how many wild animals are injured by barbed wire every day throughout the world. Another sad strike against humankind.

Some of the final strands of such wire in my territory were gathered between sessions of writing this, after Okan and Iniskim got old enough to help out with high-speed chainsaws and their big four-wheel drive Ford truck. These last remaining stretches of barbed wire were down in the river bottom part of our land, where the forest is so thick and damp that trees lay collapsed everywhere in nearly impenetrable piles, with the three strand fence mostly pinned and buried underneath. There's been no reward for this work, other than going back home with truckloads of firewood, *and* the knowledge that, from then on, our forest will have one less patch of man-made torment.

Cleaning up the countryside from past abuses helps develop a stronger bond with nature, as does the elimination of certain activities that might be seen as abuses on hindsight, such as the use of sprays and other chemical poisons. Although there are insects galore on our land, including wasps, flies and mosquitoes that sometimes annoy us terribly, plus swarms of grasshoppers that

eat up our gardens, yet we've never used insect sprays. A lot of
birds make this a major stop on their annual migration cycle, so
we get satisfaction knowing we've done nothing to bring them
discomfort or death.

*Two tipis set up on our meadow during the first years that we
were here. We camped in the nearest one, while a visiting family stayed in the other.*

7.

Beyond Hunting

Just got back from making a round trip on my old hunting trails. Today is the end of the hunting season, but I wasn't carrying a gun. Fresh white snow on the ground showed many new tracks; within ten minutes I saw the first animal, a whitetail doe, staring at me through a patch of tall, skinny pines, not certain of my intentions since the snow had let me approach so noiselessly. Before she could decide how to react, I disappeared from her sight around a brush-covered knoll, only to walk into the midst of a herd of eight elk, including a young spike bull, all looking about as surprised as I felt. The closest of them wasn't more than a stone's throw from me, steam trailing upward from her nostrils, half chewed strands of grass sticking out from her mouth. All the while, her big brown eyes beheld mine silently.

What a pleasure for this old hunter to wander those busy trails with no intention other than to see what's going on along them. Many a victim have I claimed in the past seasons along the very same route; meat to feed our family, hides to tan for moccasins and other things. Back then, all the kids in our household were small, so hunting was my job, though sometimes I brought them along for the experience. Once they got old enough to hunt I moved along to other things, like wandering trails during the final day of hunting season knowing I'd have to spill no blood. Their great-grandfather Wolf Old Man would have been proud of them, and glad for the wild food. He used to paint their faces with sacred earth paint when they were little, wishing them well with some of his prayers and songs.

We've got an old neighbor in this part of the mountains named Pete Lum, who is now of about the same vintage as Wolf Old Man was back then, in his mid-nineties. Pete lives alone in a little log house about ten miles away, as the crow flies. He's been a hunter nearly all his life, beginning as a boy, although lately his eyes have kind of given out. About the last shot he took at any-thing was when a grizzly tried to break into his place for the dog food. Pete always had a couple dozen yelping currs hanging around his place, sometimes running off to harass nearby wild-life. While the grizzly tried to break down the door, Pete held it shut with one arm and reached for his rifle with the other. Not an easy task when you're barely five feet tall! But one blast from Pete's gun and, as he himself put it, "That grizzly wasn't ever seen no more."

There's not many fellows around nowadays who've spent as much time in the wilderness as Pete. He knew a country none of us will ever see again. He first arrived in this area with his brother back when the only way of mountain travel was by foot or horse-back. Their Chinese father ran a store out in western British Co-lumbia, where he married a native woman who was their mother. Pete figures he combined skills and ways from both his parents' people in making his own living in and around these mountains. In the process he has gained respect and admiration from all who have met him.

Pete knows our family homestead well, although he probably hasn't been down here since before I was born, and that's already half a century ago. Our meadow used to be a popular camp-ground for families of Kootenay Indians, during their hunting and roaming up and down this river valley. Pete used to travel around with some of them, and that's how he got to know our place. First thing he asked me when we met, twenty-some years ago, was, "How's the trapping?"

"Trapping?" I recall asking him back, feeling as though I'd been discovered neglecting an expected duty.

"Yeah," he said pleasantly, adjusting the thick-lensed wire-rim glasses he wore back then. "Boy, we used to get some nice bea-vers and muskrats out of those ponds near you." I recall looking at him with feelings of horror, though I'm sure he never noticed. When I mumbled meekly that I hadn't actually done any trap-ping there, he looked at me with pity, as though now convinced that I was just some city-slicker fooling around in the wilderness. How could I explain to him that as a kid in Europe I always dreamed of being around peaceful and undisturbed nature.

"Well, you're missing out on a good deal," was all he could say, though later he told a mutual friend that I must have arrived with a lot of money (I didn't). To him, anyone living on the land is expected to take from it whatever there is of value, whether trees, minerals, gravel, or animal furs, same as a farmer harvesting produce or fruit.

At Pete's age, that's an understandable attitude, since there was no other way to survive in this rugged mountain country when he was young. You worked hard at it and used whatever was at your disposal. He walked along endless miles of unspoiled streams and uncut forests, often without seeing anyone else for days. Though he drove a pickup truck until not long ago and follows the world news on a big color television, it would be too much for him to try imagining what forces will threaten the survival of nature over the next century. He deserves to spend his final seasons with recollections of the past.

One of the beaver ponds between the river and our house. The large mud lodge at left has since gotten even taller. I often paddle through here quietly and get rewarded with close-up sightings of beavers, ducks, geese and other wildlife.

But those of us who are younger must surely take all the responsibility we can for preserving nature and our environment. For the longest time we left this up to a vague and barely understood government bureaucracy. Now we all need to put our thoughts and energies together to make sure our nature survives. We've constantly got to remind ourselves that it's the only one we've got!

Tranquil afternoon along the Kootenay River

8.

A Glimpse Into the Past

We knew another old timer who used to actually camp here on our meadow. Andrew Michel was an elder of the Kootenay tribe who grew up with his grandparents, living in a tipi and travelling with horses. This was around the turn of the century, before the railway had arrived, back when there were few non-natives in this valley. Andrew and his Kootenay people still travelled up and down the river using their odd-shaped canoes - with downward pointed bows - found in only one other place in the world, among a tribal people of Siberia, across the Bering Straight. Andrew was a teenager when the last steamboats battled their way up and down this wild river in an effort to supply "modern" public transportation, hauling people, supplies and gold. He knew the hidden rocks, sharp bends and sudden waterfalls where most of the steamers came to grief. He watched the "white man" arrive here, chasing the mightiest animals far into the mountains to kill them just for their horns, or running cumbersome steamboats aground. But by the time I knew Andrew Michel he was a tired old man, his people vastly outnumbered, few of them even knowing of his boyhood kind of life. The once vast wilderness of that time had been fenced in and criss-crossed with roads, much of it changed and despoiled for all time.

Andrew Michel's traditional Kootenay tribal country covered a wide range of valleys and mountains in British Columbia, Montana and Idaho. I feel fortunate to have known him, one of the last of his tribe who roamed much of that tribal region, and - most especially - one who considered our little meadow among his most intimate places. He sat and called on the spirits of his grandparents the first time I brought him here.

We had a sweatbath together, during which he addressed the various spirits of animals he'd hunted here for his family long ago, as a youth. Later, he told our kids some of the tribal legends that he grew up with, including the tale of a giant fish said to have been involved in the original making of this land, its outline still visible today in a sandy mountainside that is also a popular tourist attraction half an hour away. There was no doubt whatsoever in Andrew's mind that this was *his* country, and that his ancestors originated nowhere but in this valley, scientific "evidence" about canoe shapes and other things to the contrary. To mention the Bering Straight was asking for trouble with him. He'd get a silent, angry look on his face that somehow reminded me of the fierce and famous Genghis Kahn....

Interestingly, whereas ethnologists have been able to trace the migrations of most Native American tribes, they've found nothing to show that the Kootenay people have lived anywhere but here all along. Major evidence for migration patterns comes from the relationships of various tribes to a common language stock. In that regard the Kootenay, though always consisting of a fairly small population, have kept alive a language with its own stock, spoken nowhere else in the world.

Andrew asked me once if I liked to fish, then surprised me by pointing westward and saying, "There's a little rocky ledge out that way where you probably throw in your line." He was describing the very spot I found on my own the first time I fished around here; even when I catch nothing I feel good just to sit there and watch the river flow by, various shapes of mountains rising all around me. It is one place that has not been changed by the hands of man since the time of Andrew's youth, nor anyone's youth before then.

What has changed a lot here, according to Andrew, is the way our forest looks. "There were lots of big, tall trees" he said "with open spaces underneath." Now we have hardly any original trees left, after two thorough sessions of logging, one in the 1920's and another in the 60's. The aftermath was dense forest growth different from the natural system, allowed to grow unchecked after the cycle of natural forest fires was halted by modern methods. Thinning out the weakest trees and the most crowded places ourselves, by hand, we hope to slowly restore our forest more to the way it looked when Andrew Michel was young. Perhaps when our grandchildren are old there will again be stands of immense trees here. We must try to rectify the wrongs done to nature by previous generations whenever and wherever we can. When it comes to our environment we *must* do more than read bad stories and shake our heads about them.

9.

Squealing Elk

One of my journal entries reads, "Sunny and bright morning and all's well, except that three darned elk woke me up extra early with their thoughtless fooling around, just outside the caboose." I was being facetious, of course, but I'd written late the previous night and was hoping to sleep in, which is why I stayed in the caboose instead of down at the house with its four ambitious youngsters. When I looked out at those elk in the dawning light, one of them was acting strangely, sticking her head way up into the air while craning her neck, as if something was caught in her throat. Every once in a while she'd start jumping around wildly, though only within a small area. The other two tried to dodge and avoid collisions, but otherwise stayed nearby as if they didn't want to leave their crazy partner alone. I never did figure out what the problem with this one was. But like humans, animals also have their odd characters.

Animals are usually very protective of their young, as this next story in my journal explains. I'd gone out snowshoeing across our land when I saw a big cow elk with two calves slowly grazing up towards an open draw. Silently, and even more slowly than they, I followed at a distance; the wind was blowing strongly towards me and it had been snowing steadily for many hours. When I finally reached the top of a ridge, I was not far from them. But by then I was so cold from the slow stalking that I decided just to let them see me before heading back home. Icy snow had been blowing constantly against my face while I followed those elk into the north wind.

As soon as I stepped out into the open the cow got rather angry, while her two calves just stood and stared. She faced me, ears straight up, legs apart, watching to see what I was going to do. For lack of a better idea, I raised my left hand and waved very slowly, which made her bark once, quite loudly, at the same time stomping down with one front foot. At that I raised my other hand and waved them both, not threateningly, just slowly. She barked again and stomped with her other foot. I kept waving, so she kept barking, stomping down with alternate front feet after each bark, but otherwise doing nothing. The calves looked very uneasy, as if thinking, "C'mon mom, let's just go and leave this crazy person alone." Then suddenly they got too restless and started running around, until one of them slipped on a patch of ice hidden under the snow, causing it to fall flat on the ground. It jumped back up in an instant, but I'd never seen an elk fall like that before. After that, all three elk walked slowly away from me, while I turned and went in the opposite direction. Every once in a while I could still hear the cow barking, as if she were warning me not to change my mind, until finally her voice was lost in the snow-laden winds. It sure felt good to get back home by the hot stove to relate that experience to the family.

Four elk graze peacefully in the background while our kids play on the frame of their swings, outside our old family house. More elk were grazing on both sides of us, beyond the picture, none of them seeming to be disturbed by our presence.

10.

Running Moose

It's always exciting to stand out on our field in silence and suddenly hear loud noises somewhere in the area that may be caused by a big animal. It's taken years to learn how to identify most of them, though at night all I can do is listen, sometimes going back inside not knowing for sure just exactly *what* is wandering around nearby. If it's daytime I usually go check it out, preferring to see for myself.

So it was one early fall morning when I got to the water pump with two buckets and suddenly heard loud splashing sounds down at the pond. Ducks can be pretty noisy, especially when there's a big flock of them in the water, as two or three dive under at the same time and make a combined splashing that sounds like way more than it is. But what I heard, as I stood silently by the pump, was definitely something bigger than a couple of ducks, so I jogged across the field with my bare feet, then rushed down the slope and through a narrow strip of forest until I reached the edge of the pond, where willow brush allowed me to approach silently. On a hump of wild-mint-covered mud in the middle of the pond stood a young brown-coloured moose, busily plucking greenery out of the water, while another one stood in the shallows over by the opposite bank. In a short while a much bigger cow moose stepped out of the forest, her glossy hair virtually black by comparison. The two must have been her previous year's calves.

Slowly these two young ones drifted towards each other, stopping to graze along the way, raising their heads up from the pond frequently, allowing the water to run from their mouths, which caused the loud splashing that I'd heard. It was a classic outdoor scene, bathed in early morning light, so I took a chance that they'd stay for a while and ran back home to get a camera.

Returning as silently as I'd left, I was halfway there when I heard the splashing turn louder and more urgent, indicating that the moose were on the run. Although I was at the edge of the field, running over flat open ground instead of in shallow water and two feet of mud, by the time I reached the spot where pond and field again came together they'd already gone by, leaving only their murky trail swirling in the normally-clear water. From there the pond and field are again separated by forest, so I stayed in the open and ran as fast as I could, hoping to catch one more glimpse of this moose family. But when I finally stopped long enough to hear above my gasping breath, their loud cracking sounds came from way up ahead.

While I stood there listening, Okan caught up to me quietly, having surmised from the way I rushed in and out of the house for my camera that there was something outside worth getting up to see. As we stood there talking quietly together, the three moose suddenly reappeared, no longer on the run and apparently ready to go on with their underwater harvesting. I made my way closer very silently, camera ready in both hands, waiting to get a good, clear view. Suddenly two mallard ducks flew out from their hiding place among some reeds right in front of me, heading towards the mama moose, who immediately looked at their takeoff spot to see what had scared them. And there I was, getting my telephoto lens focused, waiting for the moose and ducks to get just a bit closer to each other for an ideal picture. Instead, all three moose moved instantly into dense brush, this time across the water from us, with the cow looking steadily back at me, but not with any sign of fear.

Okan and I were able to see those three moose once more, from quite close, but surrounded with too much brush to photograph. Instead, we stood and watched as they bent over bunches of willow branches by straddling them, then nipping off their tender tops. Their pattern of travel didn't seem to have any rhyme or reason, they just went wherever more plants were available. Maybe deep inside, their senses had them heading in a particular route, but several times they circled back and revisited the same spots, until eventually they drifted out of our view.

Another time our dogs alerted me to a big lone moose that

was crossing our field, paying no attention to the barking nor to me once I came outside for a look. The dogs were trained not to bark at deer and elk, but we see moose so seldom that they hadn't received instructions regarding them. Also I think the black hair got Tippy to thinking about bears; her bark sounded especially ferocious. I've heard of moose successfully fighting grown grizzly bears, so it's no wonder that this one didn't think much of the dogs. They in turn wisely kept their distance.

The giant of northern forests and streams, a moose like this can at times be quite dangerous.
Photo by F.J. Haynes

11.

Friends With Bushy Tails

It's hard to know when bush wolves will be having their next yodelling concert; sometimes we hear a bunch of them several nights in a row, then we don't hear any for weeks. And they definitely seem to howl more under a full moon, though I've been out on some full moon nights when the whole countryside was just totally silent.

Bush wolves have burrows galore in this area, yet I seldom see occupants in them when I walk by, or even if I stop and watch quietly for a while from a distance. Bush wolves seem to come and go like ghosts; they seldom stay in the same burrow for long; I have to study the soft sand around burrow holes carefully to determine which ones they're staying in. About one in ten, it seems, maybe even less. When one or two bush wolves pass through our meadow regularly, heading in the same direction day after day, then I know they have a family in a den nearby. This only happens for a single season at a time, then they go off and move somewhere else. I know when pups are in a burrow, because I'll see one or the other parent guarding the neighborhood every time I come by on my rounds. The guard will run a ways to catch my attention, then sit down and yelp, either warning its family, or just trying to draw me away from the den.

An old trapper once bragged to me about a golden colored bush wolf that he caught near my first homestead, along the Columbia River. This poor thing got its leg smashed in a steel trap, but was okay otherwise, the old guy said. He threw a tarp over it, wrestled it down, then tied its mouth shut with electrical tape. In that condition he then brought the animal into town, "for everybody to see." In my photo collection I've got an old postcard showing a bear being similarly treated. When I asked the trapper what he finally did with this golden animal he said, "I just shot him in the head."

The grandest bush wolf performance around here usually takes place during one of those white, silent winter nights when a half dozen or more start howling and yelping up and down along the river bottom, and on various ridge tops, within a radius of maybe three or four miles. Each one seemingly tries to outdo the other in length and loudness of yodel, some having quite deep voices and others singing eerily high.

There is a noticeable difference between them and the deep, strong, mournful howl of the bigger timber wolf, and you'd never mistake the two for each other.

There have been stories of ordinary dogs running with bush wolf packs, adopting the wild lifestyle and being in turn accepted, though I've never seen one of these myself. I did once own a dog who was half shepherd and half bush wolf - a handsome and smart fellow who was learning to be a good companion when he got in the way of a vehicle in deep snow and lost his life. Another time we had a young family staying here with us in a little cabin they built. One day, the largest of their three dogs decided he'd had enough of settled life, so he took off and disappeared without a trace. After that we sometimes heard distant dog barks mixed in with the bush wolf howlings. Then, about six months later, this errant dog suddenly stopped by to eat a bowl of food, greet his two pals and the two people who raised him, then left again just as abruptly, which was the last time he was ever seen.

One night last winter it was exceptionally cold and our field lay silently white, with the moon just a little ways past being full. Suddenly from the south end there came a slow, deep moan, like that made by an air raid siren when it first starts up. I called Beverly to come out - we'd never heard a wolf howling so close. Her first comment was, "Gee, it sounds so mournful." It went up and down slowly, then had a couple of quicker ups and downs, sometimes ending on a wavering note.

That wolf kept howling while I walked briskly across the icy meadow to our studio, where I'm doing this work - and where I also keep a tape recorder. By the time I rushed back outside with it there were *two* wolves howling. The one I'd heard first had the deeper voice and kept up the same song, while a second one now joined in each time after a few notes, sang slightly higher, and had his (or her) own tune. I wondered if they'd come around because of the meat smell; it's near the end of hunting season and in the last few days the boys shot two deer and an elk. There were enough edibles among the discarded entrails to give two wolves one fair meal.

12.

Murder Confession

Your guts are on my window, your body's on the floor,
I hit you so damned fast, you'll never know what for.
Annoying me too much, you evaded my gentle touch,
So I had to grab a weapon, using force that was too much.
Will I now go to prision, or hang for a murder done?
What'll I tell the judge, where the violence came from?
Yet I truly meant to kill you, to spill your insides out.
It all was meant to go that quick, a single one-round bout.
And no, there'll be no funeral, no mourners nor a grave,
I cannot brag of what I've done, for it wasn't all that brave.
But when a person's had enough and cannot take no more,
Don't blame them if they grab a swatter and bash more flies
to the floor.

13.

Barely Gardening

Nothing beats the outdoor garden plot as a symbol of self-sufficient living, its dark soil covered with row upon row of luscious green plants growing in the sunshine. Yet, we never bother with that kind of garden anymore. Since we don't cut the natural grass on our meadow, nor spray it for insects, we get invaded by huge hordes of grasshoppers every summer and they pretty well wipe out whatever crops we've grown at just about the time we start harvesting. There was usually one exception; apparently grasshoppers don't like the taste of potato plants, so those grew pretty good, at least until something else came and got them one year. Sudden cold weather was another problem we always had with outdoor gardens, since our frost free growing season is usually ninety days, at most, which I don't find long enough.

Nowadays our growing season is such that we only have about ninety days when we *can't* grow, while the other nine months are fairly safe. Also, we've eliminated the grasshopper problems without doing anything to our meadow at all. The solution? A passive solar greenhouse, built to take maximum advantage of sunshine on the south side, while presenting limited exposure to the cold of the north. Having now had two of these structures and seen a few others in operation, I highly recommend them to anyone planning on growing a vegetable garden, especially up in the cooler north climates such as here along the Rockies.

Beverly grew up in a family that always had a garden, so I thought she'd take charge of ours, but that didn't happen. Here's her reason: "My mom always had a nice big garden, but I learned to hate garden work because it was usually assigned to us kids as a punishment. I can still hear her saying, 'Go weed a couple of rows, you bad girl.'"

There's no shortage of gardening books and publications available for those who like written directions, but for me too much information beforehand is as discouraging as too little, making me feel insufficiently prepared, so that I tend to put the whole process off, thinking to wait until I understand everything better and have all the right materials on hand. A home business adds to my "later with the garden" schedule, though my hard working Swiss father would have said I'm just making excuses. Between the work of writing books and shipping them, I'd rather go for a long hike or a boat ride during breaks, than to labor some more by digging and pulling, or carrying dirt and water.

The kids are unanimous in saying that if we'd had running water while they were growing up they would have taken much greater interest in gardening. When we still had our regular outdoor garden along with the first greenhouse, it wasn't unusual to pour forty buckets a day and still not have everything saturated. The boys were then in their early teens and they owned a weightlifting set, with which they regularly tried to outdo each other, yet for them to pump out forty buckets full of water and pour it over the garden by hand was "too much work." I guess in hindsight I should have dropped my stubborn views and made the acquisition of a motor pump a higher priority, since the resulting gardening experience would have been worth more to the kids than my principles of keeping our life simple.

Beverly points out that, although Blackfoot culture is based on hunting and not agriculture, once her people got settled on their reservation most of them became quite adept at growing their own food. It was in the time of her own youth that this self sufficiency declined, along with other aspects of native farming and ranching, as federal government agents introduced new "plans" whereby native lands were leased to non-native ranchers, who worked more "efficiently," splitting *some* of the profits with the people afterwards. Since then, Beverly says, there has been a noticeable decline in her people's health, with a lot of diabetes, arthritis, and heart problems, not to mention the resulting social turmoil.

Okan says I should point out the financial savings that come from growing a garden, something that the young bachelor is starting to appreciate as he finds himself paying for his own meals. To maximize grocery store savings you have to plant your garden carefully so you can start to harvest early and continue into fall. What tends to happen otherwise is that your main crop ripens about the same time as everyone else's, resulting in prices at the stores so low that you wonder why you even bothered to grow anything. In that case, convince yourself that the most important reward is exactly that - food grown by yourself, pure, fresh and handy.

Since I mentioned having a second greenhouse, I should add that it forms the whole south side of our new home and studio. In fact, it's actually more of a solarium, an extension to our working area, with skylights instead of a glass roof, so that the lighting is perfect for us, and for many flowers and plants, though it's a little too dark for a good crop of vegetables. It's also a great source of added warmth, while providing fresh oxygen and earthy scents to the household air.

Our first attempt at a passive solar greenhouse is the structure seen here at left, which gave us a nine month growing season instead of three. The boys and I are watching Beverly and Star feed our chickens.
Brian Clarkson Photo

14.

Cool Clear Water

Part of the "American dream" seems to require families to let their sprinklers run for hours on end, just to keep the requisite grass lawn as green as everybody else's. Ten or fifteen minutes in the shower once or twice a day is another part of that lifestyle, with few people counting the gallons, and fewer wondering where those gallons come from.

But *I* wonder, as I hear growing rumbles from places like Arizona and California, saying they want some of Canada's water, claiming that the new Free Trade Agreement gives the U.S. unobstructed access to it. Our land lies along Canada's Kootenay River, and our lifestyle is highly dependent on that river's water levels, which have been lower than usual in recent years anyway because of several very dry seasons. One of many plans being seriously discussed by the tiny but powerful minority that covets Canadian water is to turn this Kootenay River in a different direction about twenty miles upstream from us, just where it comes down out of the Rockies and passes within half a mile of the lake that has the name and is the source of the mighty Columbia River. Connecting the two would make the Columbia all the mightier (and more $ valuable), at the same time flooding immense stretches of its naturally priceless surrounding wetlands. The process would then dry up everything along the Kootenay, including where we live. A great variety of wildlife depends on this relatively undisturbed river bottom, especially in winter when summer mountain ranges higher up disappear under deep snows.

If America needed Canadian water just for people to drink, I'm sure we'd find ways to oblige. But when I think about those vast quantities of water being wasted on lawns and in showers every day, then my compassion dries up quickly. Millions live in modern cities built over dry deserts, and those places have no right to be coveting water from other parts of our continent just because they want to keep their yards and golf courses green. Fly over Phoenix or Palm Springs sometime and you'll quickly see what I mean.

Keeping close track of my own water consumption is easy, since I pump up every drop by hand. I can tell you that an adult can get by on about two gallons a day with no difficulty. That includes drinking, bathing, hand washing etc. Maybe it takes a little more in the summer, and of course I'm not counting the water in the pond where I swim most every day when the weather allows. You'd be surprised at how little water you really *need,* when you haven't got a faucet to just let it run out of!

15.

A Place Without Cars

The quiet sanctity of our meadow means so much to me that I don't mind having to walk a quarter mile up and down a steep hill each time I want to drive somewhere in my truck. The walk is often a form of meditation, especially when I come back from town or feel wound up after a long drive. Trees and birds are always here to greet me and the fresh air is a wonderful cleanser. The rest of the family doesn't get quite so poetic about this walking up and down to reach our vehicles (I've even heard the occasional grumble!), though most of our visitors have been pretty understanding about it. We've always unlocked the gate for elders, and of course for the occasional heavy loads, like boxes of books and barrels of kerosene, not to mention cement trucks and loads of lumber. But those who leave their city homes and drive here to visit have to get out and become part of nature first, and I've always liked that.

Okan says that on looking back over the years he appreciates not having seen many cars on our meadow, but that sometimes he didn't like the extra hassle. When I asked him to explain, he said, "Like eggs falling out of grocery bags when they tore open going down the dark trail at night." Well, you've got a point there son, but just think of those eggs as cholesterol we didn't eat. Besides, this didn't really happen more than a few times during all the years here. Still, if it had been up to him, Okan would have parked right outside the house. Star says she would have compromised and parked at the edge of the woods, where cars wouldn't be so noticed but would save the hill climbing. Ah, youth!

The worst memories for Star are also of coming down from our vehicle at night after a long trip, when it was pitch black outside, and no one had a flashlight, especially when it was icy and there was no easy way to keep from slipping on the steep hill.

She adds, "I also hated the times I brought grocery bags downhill through the snow on my toboggan and they ripped apart or fell over, so that the groceries got scattered all along the trail."

Another result of the hill climbing is that we've gotten a lot of good exercise over the years just hauling our groceries and weekly mailings up and down. The toughest time I ever had with that was recently when I broke an ankle and tore some ligaments after letting Star talk me into going snowboarding with her! I needed 480 pounds of books taken from the house up to my truck by the next morning for urgent shipping when there was no one home to help, so I made three trips up and down with the toboggan, going uphill on my hands and knees each time. I used a long rope to drag the load part way up, then crawled ahead as far as I could go, hoping the load wouldn't slide back down.

A couple of friends came out from town with their kids to join us for supper one winter afternoon, and they arrived kind of late, so the sun was already down and some of the wild animals were out and about. On their way downhill after parking, they heard sounds of something big cracking on the frozen snow deeper in the forest. Their kids were babbling with excitement about it when they came in. Noises like that are heard every day around here, so we didn't think much about it. We then enjoyed a good meal and a bunch of talk; it was long after dark before they got ready to leave. Keep in mind, it's about a quarter mile hike uphill through the woods from our house to the parking area.

Suddenly the mama of this bunch remembered that and began to voice her concerns. "What about those animals out there," she wondered nervously. Her husband had grown up in "the bush" himself, so he showed no pity in front of the crowd as he teased his wife about how many such animals there might be, how big, and of what kind. At first she thought he was joking, but after a while she was no longer sure. Nor were their kids, whose frightened faces only added to the mother's fears. Finally she concluded that they should all stay a little longer." We'll wait until whatever it is goes away," she said hopefully.

"Goes away, are you kidding?" somebody joked. "By now it's already smelled your tracks, so it'll wait all night behind a tree until you go back up!" The poor woman was ready to cry, but all she could say was, "Really??" I finally brought out our .22 rifle and fired a few shots into the air, assuring her that any wild animals in the area will now have cleared out, so she bravely followed her husband into the darkness, their two kids trailing so close behind that the silhouettes were all as one. Oddly enough, about fifteen minutes later I went back outside for my last "breath of fresh air," so to speak (or "to water my horses," as old Indians liked to say). In the process I spooked up a whole bunch of elk just 50 feet from the house. Those were probably the animals she'd heard on the way down, though it was a good thing she didn't notice that I was wrong in saying the gunshots had scared everything away.

Another time a young city couple showed up, wanting to "meet the author" and so forth. It was early winter, but they were dressed more for going to a theatre down the street than for driving way out into the woods. I've been stuck on foot a few times in bad weather, so I know how quickly the presence of thick jackets and good hats can be appreciated. They had on low shoes that let the snow in, with soles made for sidewalks, not steep trails. Luckily they were more thoughtful about their baby, which was wrapped up in a thick blanket. They left again after a while, assuring us that they needed no help to get back up to their car, though perhaps I should have known better. I did send a couple of the boys to lead the way, because they seemed unsure about the route of the trail. When the kids got back down they told us how the woman had bravely tried to keep up with her husband, who apparently wanted to show that he could go uphill quicker than a couple of young boys. They said there was a sudden squeal from behind, then the "thunk" of a body falling to the ground. By the time the boys turned to look, there lay the mama, sideways on the trail, while her bundled up baby was rapidly rolling back down the hill. Thank heavens this turned out alright, though there were some pretty horrendous possibilities.

Speaking of clothing, or its lack of, maybe the most singular visitor in that regard was our hardy friend Siegfried, who showed up from Germany by plane and bus one late winter, then walked in from the highway on our snowbound road *barefooted*! On his back he carried a sleeping bag, tent, and most of his worldly possessions, but hardly a heavy jacket, nor long johns at all. He said people weren't born with shoes, so he would try to do without them. I had to admire his fortitude, since he neither complained about the cold nor did he hesitate doing his share of the duties, including the chopping of wood. But eventually he did start wearing a pair of moose hide moccasins, in themselves still not providing nearly the warmth and protection of modern socks and boots, but certainly better (for us) than having to look at his pink feet melting the snow around wherever he stood, his skin covered by scrapes from the ice, rocks and sticks.

16.

Good Medicine

Sometimes I wish I had an encyclopedic knowledge of herbs and plants, along with their many varied native uses. Not only has my home been surrounded by such plants for the past 25 years, but as the author of books with titles like "Good Medicine" and "Life in Harmony with Nature," it seems that I should have been a much more serious student. A couple of our family's closest tribal elders were considered leading healers and medicine people in the Blackfoot Confederacy.

Thus I've I watched old Pat Weaselhead untying his various cloth sacks containing herbal medicines, mixing special blends of their contents for his family and ailing friends, boiling it in cups sometimes right on our stove. When my 97-year old teacher and friend Willie Scraping White died in 1974, a little suitcase he used for ceremonial paraphernalia was passed on to me by his family, and among the things in it were bags of dried plants. But being a medicine man of that sort is serious business, requiring a lifetime of study and devotion, plus a long-term commitment not only from the healer but also the patients. It's been my feeling, learned from both these wise men, that many people nowadays "fool around" with herbs and the process of healing, sometimes making up remedies of their own, then attributing special magic powers and sensational cures to them. Although both these old men were life long native doctors whose skills were widely known, neither ever claimed to have cures for such major ailments as cancer, heart disease or diabetes. Nor did they attempt curing such ailments, especially on people just passing through their country, the kind of people who try one thing today and another tomorrow. The patients these men treated were lifelong friends and relatives, so the healing and curing energies always flowed both ways.

Native healing involves faith and prayer along with medicinal plants. To become a doctor in Blackfoot tradition you need "divine inspiration," for lack of a better term. The songs and rituals come through dreams of significance or in unusual visions. You don't just say, "I'm going to study and get myself a medical license." You need this divine invitation in the first place. And that means far more than just dreams made up in someone's idle thoughts; it concerns dreams that enter subconscious minds already culturally prepared through lifelong faith and associations. However, since life itself keeps changing, it must be expected that the ways of healing change too. There are a great many new medicine men and women attempting to serve an ever greater circle of patients, while faith in the ways of nature continues to grow stronger in all parts of modern society. Some Native American healers travel to other continents nowadays, doing their work, while in turn healers from foreign tribes have made their way to North America, usually finding receptive audiences. Over the years a few of these people have visited us here, and it's been gratifying to witness this growth of international nature-orientation.

But I'm stumped when I get letters from strangers asking for help in curing some serious ailment. I have yet to witness any example of magic curing with my own eyes, and certainly have no such remedies myself. Many books, including some of mine, have lists of wild plants and some of their medicinal uses. In Blackfoot culture these would be called "everybody's medicines," meaning plants whose basic uses are well known and don't require further spiritual enhancement to use. An example of that is wild mint, which is widely known to soothe the stomach and chest. Also the oregon grape, which has value as a diuretic. Beyond that, recommending particular herbal practitioners would be risky, since some are much better than others, while a few are mostly interested in enhancing their own egos (and bank accounts), rather than in truly helping people to use nature for healing.

My own preference when it comes to physical ailments is self-healing. It's surprising how well our bodies are equipped to heal themselves, if we only give them a chance. It's so easy to reach for an aspirin when a headache comes, but I prefer to figure out what caused it, then to change what I'm doing, and finally to "ride it out", perhaps adding a self-massage, especially if the headache was caused by stress. So many everyday ailments are simply warning signals from our bodies that we're not doing something right. The solution is to change the cause, not to look for a cover-up in the medicine cabinet.

We do have our own collection of drug store "quick-remedies," which get used to varying degrees in our household. But we also have roots and herbs on hand that we've found useful over the years. If there's a *serious* ailment we don't hesitate to visit our family doctor, who also happens to be a friend. I admire people who say they never take any pills at all (my own yearly average is only about two or three); I also admire those who say they can solve *all* their ailments with just natural brews. But even the venerable Willie Scraping White left space in his ceremonial suitcase for various drug store prescriptions, along with a bottle of Pepto-Bismol and a little jar of Vicks. In town he had a favorite doctor who took care of the things he couldn't remedy himself.

Willie Eagle Plume was another of our family elders who liked coming over from the prairies to spend time in our mountain home. He was very knowledgeable in traditional Blackfoot ways and eager to see them passed on to younger generations. Here is how he described a few of the wild plants gathered and used by his father Eagle Plume, a great-grandfather of Beverly's, a noted doctor and ceremonialist among the Bloods at the start of this century.

"I will tell you a little story of how my father used to get his doctoring medicines together. For instance, if someone was hemorrhaging from the mouth, he would use a combination of Gros Ventre scent (western meadow rue), sweetgrass, and white clay. The Gros Ventre scent had to be green. My mother would put these plants in the oven for a long time, feeling and checking them every once in a while. When they were very soft she would take them out and crumble them into a piece of buckskin. When she was finished, they looked like black pepper.

"There was this white man we called Mountain Chief. He was spitting blood and he asked my father to make a brew for him. My father made a small brew and prayed while he boiled it. Then he told the man to drink it with the leaves in it. He told him, "Don't lie to me. Tell me the truth if you like it and if it works for you." He drank it. A couple of days later he was much better. That man gave my father a horse, some cash, and other things for curing him.

"Back when I used to ride horses, one time a horse fell on me. My knee swelled up. My father told my mother to get some thorns from a rose bush and bake them. She baked them. He pushed some of the hot thorns into my injured leg. I thought my leg was going to break! He put a long stick into the fire, and while it was burning he painted the thorns with sacred yellow paint and sacred black paint. Then he took the glowing red stick and heated the thorns, which burned right down to my skin. My leg felt like it was being held by something powerful. I couldn't move it at all. The next day I was able to move my leg, but my father said, "Today we will have the treatment one more time." After the second treatment, the swelling went down and I was able to walk. I guess that was a form of what they call acupuncture today.

"Now let me tell you about some of the different things that grow. For instance, the 'man-sage' (prairie sage) is used by men, the 'woman-sage' (pasture sage) by women. If a man has any kind of bad luck, he will use the prairie sage to cleanse the evil from his body. If a relative dies, a man will make incense with the prairie sage and rub it over himself to cleanse his body. They are pure growths from nature, so they can clean away unpure things. If a man is going to have a sweat lodge, he will sit on the man-sage and he will chew some. This will purify him.

"There are all kinds of uses for this man-sage. When they went on war raids they would carry some leaves to chew on, so they wouldn't get out of breath. They chewed it for the same reason when swimming. If a man has smelly feet he will put some leaves in his moccasins to make the smell go away. He will boil some and wash his hair in it. If his nose is bleeding, he will chew it and put it in his nose to stop the blood. If he has body odor, he will put some under his arms and between his legs and the smell will go away. If he has the itch, he will boil some and put it on whatever place is itching. A man will put in a few leaves of man-sage in any kind of curing brew to purify it. In the Old Days, men put bunches of man-sage in the nose and mouth of their kill to purify it. Also it makes the meat taste good

"A woman uses woman-sage in the same way. A handsome woman will bathe with it and use it in her hair. For an easy birth, she will chew on it. She will use it for perfume and to keep herself from sickness.

"My father always prayed while picking medicine plants. He kept all his curing medicines tied up in little buckskin pouches. There was no writing on them; he used different-colored beads to tell apart the few bags he didn't know by the way they looked and smelled. Sometimes he would show them to me and say, "I will use this for coughing, and this for hemorrhaging, and this for swelling." He put sage in with them to keep them pure. My father taught me a lot of his medicines, but I have lost most of them. Nobody was interested, so I have forgotten them."

17.

Nature Kids

Having small children in the family is no excuse for staying away from nature, nor for staying in the city instead of taking up country life, *if* that's what you really want to do. When Beverly and I came to this homestead we brought four-year old Wolf and his new brother Okan who was just 6 weeks old. Had I been able to arrange it, I would have delivered him myself, here on this land and in a tipi. But a certain mother-in-law threatened the warpath if I dared to subject her one and only daughter to such "risky and primitive methods." To back up her stand, she told me once again the family legend of the grandmother who died in her own tipi after complications from childbirth, and also of another family child lost when a tipi midwife cut its umbilical cord too short. Besides, in Blackfoot customs the husband stays away from his mate at birthing and doesn't play midwife.

Beverly says it was no harder being a mom to growing babies way out here in the wilds than it would have been in town, or back on her well-populated reservation. We were certainly lucky to have had no serious emergencies while living here through the years. One of the more memorable incidents was the time I had to put a few stitches in Okan's head after he fell and cut himself open. Another time I did the same for the son of a friend when a tin stove pipe fell on his head and left a bleeding gash.

Our family doctor kept me supplied with a few basic emergency materials, including thread and needles to sew up sudden wounds. Beverly says that raising kids successfully in nature requires mainly common sense, the most important of which is to feed them well. She feels strongly that "You are what you eat." "Making sure they're always properly dressed is also very important, and of course seeing that they have a safe and warm place to sleep. We didn't worry much about what things our kids might miss out on, knowing that our life in nature would make up for most of it. As they grew older we were sometimes disappointed with the choices they made (myself more so than Beverly) but we tried to let them choose whenever possible, as long as there was no conflict with our basic family lifestyle.

I will take this opportunity to urge most strongly that all new parents consider a commitment to keep television out of their home while children are growing up. While this piece of technology has many wonderful aspects (you can't hardly get me away from one, once I check into a hotel room), it often impacts severly on a family's inter-relationships, becoming the central focus of the household. Television can take away a child's inspiration to be creative and replace it with devilish influences that may affect them for the rest of their lives. It makes us forget that everyday life can be pretty good entertainment by itself.

"Do flowers buzz when bees take juice out of them?" oldest son Wolf once asked me when he was still pretty small. Another time he was wandering around the cabin, looking kind of lonely, so we asked what was the problem. "I wonder where's my cat?" he said, on the verge of tears. "I think it's out tomcatting around," answered Mama, trying to cheer him. To that his eyes lit up, as he replied, "No, I think he's out in the woodshed, watching *TV!* "

In those days, asking him an earnest question often got strange replies. One time he was across the room from me playing with his toys when I heard something crash loudly to the floor. I asked him what it was, but he gave me no reply. So I asked again, then a third time, but still he said nothing. Finally I got up and went over to have a look, then demanded to know, "Why aren't you answering me?" He turned his head towards me with a very disturbed face and said, "Because I don't like the way that question is worded."

Another time he had been aggravating me by repeating a certain noise, so I finally asked him why he didn't stop. "Cause that's the only way," came his reply. When I complained about his messy room and asked why stuff was scattered everywhere, he shrugged his shoulders and said, "Cause the Great Spirit put it there."

Reading bedtime stories has been a custom in our family since

Wolf was old enough to understand them, and it continued until the last of our kids turned into a teenager. I had just finished "The Ogre's Three Golden Hairs," when Wolf said to me, "Gee, these books are a hassle." When I asked him why, he replied, "Because they always get finished."

When he was about five we were getting dressed for a trip into town and Mama was trying to rush him for being so slow. She looked down with disgust and said to him, "You've got your moccasins on the wrong feet!" To that he answered very seriously, "I don't got no other feet to put them on."

Beverly was cleaning the kitchen one day while the kids were, as usual, playing all around. When this used to happen to our adopted grandma Mary Ground, she'd say, "you kids get out from underfoot!" Our kids didn't on this day, which led to this brief exchange. Iniskim had stopped by his mom just as she was wiping the dust from our fire extinguisher. When she accidentally pushed on the release lever, there was an instant "whoosh," which startled her so much that she jumped back and said, "Oh God!" An instant later Iniskim looked down at himself and saw that he'd been sprayed with white foam, to which he also instantly and earnestly said, "Oh God!" We all got a big laugh, though he didn't join us until after the shock wore off.

Another time when Iniskim was about four, he asked his mom while eating, "If I squeeze my stomach and make my food come up, will I get smaller?"

About a year later, while his mama was pregnant with Star, he threatened one day:"I'm gonna pull out your belly button so that the baby will come out! "

I have lots of notes about things that Star said; it was funny to watch her being influenced by everyone older, as she was then our youngest. For instance, one time lunch consisted of a bean and onion salad made by a visiting friend who used lots of oil and curry powder. It looked and smelled unlike the food we usually eat, so the boys refused to touch theirs, but I decided to be brave and eat mine. Star soon said that she didn't like hers either, so I tried to be encouraging. "Eat it and you'll get tough," I told her, then added, "all Indians eat this kind of salad to get tough."

She looked up at me with disdain and said in a real serious voice: "Where did you get an idea like that - did you read it in a book or something?" Guess I got told; by a three-year old, yet!

She awoke one morning to a wet bed, which really bothered her once she'd learned to use a plastic pail that was appropriately pink. Around that era the boys used to tease her by calling her a "Mohawk," so that morning I said she was a "Mohawk wetty beddy." This really bugged her, but it made her mama and me laugh. Later, at my desk, I pulled out my journal and told her that I was going to write down her new nickname so that we'd always know it. She said nothing at first, but went off for pen and paper, then busied herself trying to write "Adolf." She thought this was *my* "nickname" and that it would thus annoy me. When she learned that it's not, she produced another piece of paper and said she would write "something else bad" about me.

Just before his ninth birthday Okan said, "For a present I want to get nine dollars!" One-year-younger brother Iniskim said immediately, "I'm gonna get eight!" To this, two year old Star added, "For *my* birthday, I'm not gonna get ate!"

Okan asked me one time, "How old is that girl that lives in that little house in Browning?" He must have been about four or five, so I tried to think of which girl in that age group he meant. Finally I had to ask him, so he explained, "You know, that girl that still knows how to write." Gee, which one could that be? Then he added that "she stays alone in an old house in town," so I knew he meant Mary Ground, a "girl" of 97 and a highly respected Blackfeet elder. A week before that she'd surprised Okan and me during a visit when she wrote out a neat note for the owner of the local mercantile store, asking him to give us Bull Durham tobacco as her contribution to an upcoming ceremony we were having. Few old time Indians of her generation were able to write very much, so she made a strong impression on Okan's mind.

While standing by my desk one time when she was about four, Star said, "I'm starting not to like my cheeks." When I asked her why she said, "Because Wolf always grabs them!" Then she pushed against them with the palms of her hands and asked, "If I do this will they go in?"

One fall our three boys had an interesting visitor, a small fellow, who was a couple of years older than them and wore blond braids. This guy had grown up in the outdoors with several brothers and figured that he was pretty brave, though he'd had few actual tests so far in life.

He and Wolf decided they were going "wilderness camping" by themselves. Wolf was only eight, so Beverly asked me to talk them out of it. I told them that bears in this area like to eat little boys for dessert after supper, but that didn't scare our hero, who said he'd just climb up a tree. When I told him that they climb trees too he said, "they can't climb *small trees,* so that's what I'll do!"

Eventually the two settled for building themselves a little village with old boards on a former millsite that is near the edge of our woods, but still within sight of the house. That gave me an idea which I quickly put into action, though not before alerting Beverly so she could watch the results from a distance.

Grabbing one of our tanned buffalo robes and an old magazine, I ran in a roundabout way until I was just a few yards above those busy boys. Then I got down behind some bushes on my hands and knees, draped the buffalo hide over myself, rolled up the magazine, and began grunting and growling through it fairly loudly. At first there was no reaction so I thought they didn't fall for my trick. I kind of jumped up and down a bit, then grunted some more. Suddenly I heard the sounds of their escape, so I stood partway up to watch them running helter skelter across the open meadow towards the house. Later they said they'd been working with their tools, constructing their little lumber buildings, when they "saw a brown thing moving." Our visitor at first dismissed it as being "just an old horse," but when he looked again *and* heard my noises, he suddenly shouted, "no it isn't!" and jumped up to run away. Wolf, being smaller and afraid of getting left behind, dropped my hammer and nails, while the friend kept his until he tripped over some broken branches and fell, after which he had nothing left in his hands either.

By the time I made my way inconspicuously back to the house, Wolf was nearly in tears and his friend was talking excitedly to Beverly, his eyes still big with fear. I pretended to take great interest in their tale, then asked them what they did with my tools. When they confessed to having left them behind, I insisted they go back and get them. At that point Wolf's tears overflowed, while his friend protested, saying, "Only a Tom *Fool* would go back there!" We let them dwell on this for a while before finally telling them the truth. I think the experience helped them to see nature on a more realistic scale.

This same kid's dad had written from California after reading some of my books, thinking that I was trying to get a new "tribe" together. He wanted to ride clear up here on horseback with his whole family, which would have been a singular effort among the many visitors we got. But they rode only as far north as Oregon before having to give up the horses for lack of feed and too much legal hassle, after which they continued their journey aboard a Greyhound bus instead. They arrived at the Canadian border in mountain man gear of leather, wearing breech cloths, leggings, and long hair, so the immigration people sent them away, telling them they lacked enough money to have a good visit, not believing that the dried food supplies in our friend's baggage would really sustain them as they claimed.

Unfortunately, *they* didn't intend for it to, either. The man of the family told me by mail that he figured to feed his family in large part by hunting all year round, though he could not have done so legally. The last thing we wanted around here was a foreign mountain man roaming the woods in our region with a gun. We admired the fellow for his strong convictions, but were sure relieved that he didn't end up here to create problems for the rest of us.

I guess it's common for the youngest member of a family to make extra efforts at proving bravery, especially if he's a boy among boys who live in the outdoors. One time when Iniskim was 12 and Okan 13 the three of us were at a campground along Cutbank Creek, just inside Glacier National Park in Montana. We were taking a break from two ceremonies we'd come to attend among friends and relatives on the adjoining Blackfeet Reservation. Since upper Cutbank Creek is known as grizzly country, the boys wanted to go for a walk so we could have a look, before we settled down in our camp for the night. So we headed up towards the mountains on a well marked trail, walking silently and on alert. As we left open country to enter dark forest, a sign warned us that the trail was closed to human traffic four miles ahead due to "grizzly danger." At that point normally-brave Iniskim stopped and said, "Let's go on back," as it was now getting dusk. I told Okan, "I think he lost his bravery in bits and pieces along the way." When Iniskim denied that, I told him, "Alright then, lead the way for one more mile and we'll all go back." Taking the challenge, he led off without another word. After a ways, the narrow trail rounded a bend and passed by a large tree, where I motioned to Okan so that we both stepped silently behind it. In the moments just before, I had taken care to cough once or twice and shuffle my feet so he'd know I was still there, then we watched to see what he would do. He went on for quite a ways into the growing darkness before he realized that he was alone, at which point he turned and quickly came back, looking neither left nor right, as if he didn't care where we were. We let him pass by in silence, then fell back into line just as we'd been before. When we got out of the woods near the campground he stopped for a pause at which point Okan said, "Now he's going to get his bravery back."

When Star was about six she asked me real seriously one time, "Am I two-faced?" I said no, but she persisted, asking, "Am I just a little bit two-faced?" I told her, "Not the way I know you, not at all." She paused for a minute or so then said, mostly to herself, "Well, I think I'm just a little tiny bit two-faced."

At that point I asked her, "Do you know what two-faced is?" She said, "Yeah, it's when a friend be's good to you, until another friend shows up, then gangs up and be's bad to you." One of Star's earliest observations on the nature of human relationships.

Around that same time Star and I were being affectionate one afternoon, so I told her "anything that's mine is also yours." She was real happy about that. In the evening at the supper table I overheard her tell one of her brothers that she's got enough money to buy a certain toy they'd been discussing. By then I'd forgotten about our earlier encounter, so I curiously asked from where she'd gotten the money for this toy. With an innocent look she told me, "Remember, you said anything that's yours is mine." I swallowed hard, nodded my head, and wondered just how literally she was going to take me on that. I noted in my journal that I'd have to let her go however far she wanted to, "even to bankruptcy," but I also added that I had total faith in my kids not to abuse a situation like that. I may have complained regularly about their seemingly foolish money spending. (I think most parents do.....) but I've felt all along that our kids understood the basic power of money pretty well. It's certainly a major force on humankind and the world, which is strange since it seems so totally without life or spirit. Incidentally, Star still reminds me sometimes to this day that what's mine is hers, though I can say with appreciation that she never once abused it (nor did she end up buying that toy back then).

Some of our friends and relatives couldn't keep themselves from wondering aloud now and then over the years whether our kids would grow up to follow our way of life, or to resent what they missed out on by being raised way out here. One old Swiss aunt of mine was particularly concerned that descendants of her family should live like "uneducated primitives" out in the wilderness, though I think she made up her mental picture from visits to the Amazon on television, rather than by looking at the snapshots I sent her. When I asked the three nearly grown kids who were home for supper this evening, they agreed unanimously that they consider themselves as well educated, grade for grade, as any of their friends. There's certainly nothing "primitive" about the snazzy clothes they wear these days, nor their appearances in society, otherwise.

One of the first signs I got that our kids would not necessarily follow my wilderness footsteps was when Wolf got into his midteens. As the oldest, he had to break the barriers, test my limits, take the chances by introducing "new" ideas. Like the time I came home from a long journey to find the wall and ceiling around his bed covered with magazine pages and posters showing all manner of "wild looking" guys, his favorite singers and bands, mostly with weird or creepy names. They all seemed to share long tousled hair styles of various colors, plus the desire to bare their chests, somewhat covering the rest of their bodies with various pieces of impractical looking clothing, much of it apparently shredded with scissors on purpose, else made from material previously attacked by moths and mice. Bizarre facial make-up and/or expressions seemed to have replaced the pretty-boy smiles and styles of singers in the past. Wow, is this how my sons will react to life in harmony with nature, I found myself wondering. But once the initial shock wore off, I surprised myself by not really caring after all, figuring every generation of kids have their interests and expressions, yet most end up doing something worthwhile with their deeper selves once they grow up and get beyond the distractions of entering maturity. I decided not to worry unless he got to be about 25 or 30 and was then still laying around on his bed with magazines and cats, a walkman playing noisy stuff into his brain through a pair of padded earphones.

To my initial dismay, our boys early on showed keen interest in anything motorized, or on wheels, my example of bringing us here to live "simply" having little apparent influence. To the contrary, the lack of these around here may have made motors all the more appealing. On the other hand my father worked all his life with wheels, motors and machines, whereas his father also lived simply, working at home as a tailor, walking everywhere or taking a train. My oldest son is the fourth to carry the same first name, two Adolfs liking motors and two of them not.

Okan was the first to bring us grief with this motor enthusiasm, as he borrowed his brother's motorcycle one day for a roar down the quiet highway, which seemed safe enough. My biggest concern whenever they had motorcycles was the rough dirt road between the highway and here, full of deep ruts, and very slippery in any kind of rain. There have been a few minor spills on this road, but none were so near to disaster as Okan's highway crash, when he suddenly found his front wheel caught in a wide crack running the same way as he in the pavement. Lucky for him, nothing worse happened than some deep body gouges, plus dents on the motorcycle and the destruction of his pants and a nice new jacket. I hear the nature boy was rolling along at something in the neighborhood of a hundred per when he lost control and crashed. Fortunately he was alone and there was no other traffic.

Though we never had any serious accidents while the kids were growing up, we certainly had our share of scares. One evening we were all sitting around the table playing cards except for Wolf, who was then about 17 and preferred his own games (reading a Playboy magazine while laying on his bed, that particular time). Suddenly he got up, intending to step outside, but instead made a faint "ohh!" sound and keeled forward, right into Star's arms. She thought he was being "cute" so she started to hug him, but let go when she felt him pulling away. Instead, he collapsed face first into a bunch of empty clay cups that were sitting at the edge of the table.

My initial concern was that he cut his face, so I grabbed him instantly to check, but he slipped out of my hands too and went right on to the floor, looking pale and totally disoriented. Before we could think, everyone's panic button was pushed. I knelt down to hold him, asking if he was alright. "I'm not sure," he said after a pause, looking at me very strangely. A few minutes passed before he began to come out of it. We all kind of sat there, numb and silent, staring while he recovered. Gulp!

Another time Iniskim came charging up the steps of my caboose all out of breath and looking scared, saying only, "Mama has to drive Wolf to the hospital; he hurt his eye." So I grabbed my jacket and hat, then rushed up to the house full of concern. By the time I got there, the victim was being led from the house by his mom while he held a towel over his face. It turned out the boys were visiting and 11-year old Iniskim decided to "fool around" with a BB gun which, as in many cliches of this sort, "wasn't supposed to be loaded." It was, and he fired, catching Wolf right in the face. It was foolishness for sure, but it taught them a powerful lesson that they haven't forgotten, nor have Beverly and I. Luckily it turned out that the BB hit Wolf's lower eyelid just at the edge; a fraction further and the consequences for his eye would have been tragic. Instead, it just looked wickedly bruised for a long time and gave Iniskim a sad image of his big brother to see and think about.

Our biggest relief was that he'd been handling the BB gun, not one of our hunting rifles. Like sons in most rural households, our boys grew up with guns always at hand. But on discussing this, they were sure that if there had been a heavy caliber rifle in their midst they would have all acted much more seriously to begin with. I solved the problem by confiscating every gun in the house, except for one that Wolf owned, figuring it wouldn't be fair to punish him when he was already suffering.

One thing that periodically disturbs the sanctity of our home is chickens. Right now there's a flock of nine (which started with ten, may the missing one r.i.p.), and these red-feathered egg layers are putting in their fourth winter around here, which in the chicken world is getting pretty old. They were given to Star, so they've become her fond pets, and even if their production has dropped to just one or two eggs a day (more when the weather's warmer), she won't hear of us having a chicken dumpling stew or anything like that.

But the boys sure managed to get her rooster. Somebody she knew had a spare one, a good looking fellow that she claims was "bold and aggressive," though the boys say he was just "plain arrogant and annoying," particularly his crowing, which was loud and in an odd voice. Says Iniskim: "That darned rooster would romp on the chickens all day and then spend half the night crowing besides. I don't know how he stayed alive." We noticed that elk came out onto the field much less than usual, so we suspected they didn't like the rooster either. Around here, that's the death sentence for anything, since elk get priority; but Star still wouldn't hear of it.

Well, one weekend the boys came home at some wee hour of the morning when that rooster started crowing loudly, having appointed himself to the duty of "ranch watchman." According to Iniskim, Okan swore aloud, "that's it - this is the night," whereupon he charged into the chicken house with murder on his mind. But when he couldn't see in the dark, he decided to forego the sentence. He was about to step back outside when suddenly that dumb rooster crowed right in his face. It shouldn't have done that!

18.
Lucky Ladybug

Do you know what's so lucky about a ladybug? It's the only bug that gets people to respond with feelings of affection; it's the only one that doesn't get swatted or stomped on sight. Something about this bumbling polka-dotted creature makes even little girls willing to pick them up with their bare hands and croon, "Isn't it cute?"

Today there was one crawling up a tomato plant in the greenhouse next to where I like to sit. I watched, spellbound, as this representative of a world wide tribe of beloveds fastidiously went about his business, which was? I don't know; couldn't make any sense out of this little busybody during the fifteen minutes or so that I watched. The ladybug is one grand champion of greenhouse and garden pest control. Many people pay good money to get a little box of these critters from some ladybug kennel, though the ones in our greenhouse just came on in for free.

Smiling little girls probably don't realize that ladybugs are actually predators! Vicious killers of other life forms; ruthless and efficient assassins of fellow bugs and things. Instead of hosting lucky symbols, our greenhouse has been taken over by a deadly gang of murderers. The one I was watching from my chair was probably just acting dumb so I wouldn't suspect what was back on his seemingly wobbly trail. The remains of victims, bits and crumbs of insect life left in the hurried quest for more. I'm harboring psychobugs; should I contact the National Enquirer? No telling what they could do with an idea like that!

It surprised me to realize that without thinking I've become very fond of dragonflies. As a boy I thought they were scary; I assumed they had a vicious bite, and besides that their bulging eyes looked ugly. But down here along the river bottom where we live they've become a part of our summer life - not a day goes by without seeing their glittering wings flit past my window, accompanied by a loud busy buzzing. The buzzing is like background music to their constant movement, pleasant to the ears, much more so than the incessant scratching of grasshoppers and similar other bugs, with movements that are graceful and appear to have purpose. And dragonflies seem totally undisturbed by human presence, showing neither fear nor aggression. I once sat down at our dock to sunbathe, mesmerized while a big blue dragonfly sat on the end of my nose for a good twenty minutes, the two of us staring at each other eyeballs to eyeballs. Those eyes that I used to think were so ugly now seem very mysterious to me instead. Round and patterned, as if wearing a pair of insect shades. A cool insect, that would be a good way to describe my feelings about them. I'm surprised Walt Disney never made one into a cartoon character; a fearless warrior; a cool dude. Imagine what an artist could do with those mandibles! No wonder I used to think they were scary - the one that sat so long on my nose looked like he could reach down and pierce my lip, or even my hand, if I were dumb to reach for it. Yet I've never heard of anyone getting bitten by a dragonfly, other than the ordinary household fly, which is when those big mandibles do their vicious work.

But then the normal fly must surely be a damned thing anyway; what other purpose does it have but to torment? Crows eat dead things too, but they're not so ugly about it. Besides, there's no dead things around our household, so why do flies keep bothering us? Always blackmailing us with the threat of a sickness or disease. If that's not damned, nothing is....

Then there's the minnow, another creature that apparently finds the human race fascinating. The only freshwater fish that comes *to* me when I go down to our river, instead of hiding away (like the whitefish and trout). Maybe minnows come towards me because they know that while I'm around there'll be no trout....

Some people go to a lot of trouble to experience special cleansings for their bodies. But how many of you have been cleansed by a school of minnows? Always friendly anyway, there are times when several hundred of them will nuzzle my body, all over, picking off minute minerals, I suppose. In the process they give me a tingling as if I were being touched by a thousand tiny electric wires. Magic caresses in the wilderness. Will there be minnow cleansing spas in the future, do you suppose?

19.

Home Schooling

We felt right from the start of our "homestead life" that we could teach our kids here at home, instead of sending them off to school, thereby having more influence on their values and upbringing, not to mention less outside distraction to our cultural life in nature. It helped that we both had classroom experience as teachers, if only for short periods, though we don't think that was necessary for making our home schooling efforts a reasonable success.

Back in the seventies, when our kids were young, I almost had an anarchist's outlook on schooling, having the most degrees in the family and the strongest dislike for the regimented system they represented. I might have settled for just teaching our boys how to "hunt, draw and whittle," feeling (even to this day) that any fellow (or gal) proficient in those three can make a decent living anywhere.

On the other hand, Beverly would sometimes have preferred to send the kids to regular school on a bus, even though we're about three unplowed miles from the lonely highway where it would have stopped. She grew up around that style of country schooling and places more value on its social benefits than I do. So we compromised, keeping them at home, but also following a regular schooling schedule, if only for two or three hours a day instead of all morning and afternoon.

With my lack of enthusiasm for anything that reminded me of classrooms, Beverly took over the "book learning" of our home schooling, while I handled lessons that concerned the outdoors, such as hiking and hunting, boating and fishing, or just watching for tracks while cutting firewood and hauling it home for the stoves. It didn't take long for them to start learning some of their outdoor lessons alone.

"At first I just worked on the basic 3-R's, since we hadn't actually made a teaching plan beforehand," recalls Beverly. "It wasn't that hard, with Wolf as my only student. One day I visited the principal of the nearest elementary school and asked if there were any spare books I could use. To my surprise he gave me a whole bunch, plus a lot of helpful suggestions, and even an invitation to bring the kids by for testing.

"Being well educated has long been a goal pushed in my parents' household, so I eventually gave in to their pressures and applied for more formal help with our kids' education. I got this through British Columbia's correspondence school program, which provided all the material needed for the various courses of each grade, even microscopes and glass slides for science. When a lesson was completed, we sent it back to them for marking. Some of the teachers who did the marking wrote personal notes to the kids, even exchanged pictures with them, so the schooling took on a lot of personality.

"A few years ago this provincial program was decentralized, so that we got a closer office half a day's drive from our home, where students, teachers and parents meet twice a year, discuss the schooling, swim and have other activities together, giving them all something to look forward to. The first year there were just a few students, but it doubled by the following meeting and since then it's grown every year. Whereas most people used to find us unusual for teaching our children at home, a lot are now getting turned off by the public school systems, so that home schooling is becoming much more popular."

"Ours would go along well for a time, then we'd reach a plateau where the kids would be bored by all of it. This would annoy me and make the whole process quite unpleasant. I guess it was at these times that I threatened to just send them off on a school bus the next season, but I always changed my mind, and now I'm glad that I did. These interruptions happened most often at the time of 'cabin fever,' in late winter when the weather was not good for playing outside and the short cold days had gone on long enough. After a break to visit my parents, or go to a city, I'd come back home feeling energized and ready to continue. You can imagine how proud I was of my first graduate, when

Wolf received his Grade 12 diploma. It verified our belief that children could learn their basic education at home just as well as in a crowded classroom. But believe me, it helps to have one parent there at all times to oversee that the schooling gets done."

Okan says home schooling was definitely a continual test of discipline, both for the family and for the individual student. "An undisciplined family could run into a real problem," he warns. "Once a student gets too far behind and lacks motivation, it becomes very hard and discouraging to try catching up. Using myself as an example, early on when we switched from my mom's home-made curriculum to correspondence courses, I was put back a couple of grades, and because of that I always felt somewhat discouraged and wished I was in my regular grade. Sometimes I found it embarrassing when people away from home asked about our schooling. But because my mom consistently pushed me ahead, I continued through the courses."

Beverly points out that whenever the kids got really discouraged she had a conference with the correspondence school principal, who came out here to visit regularly anyway. Upon reviewing the situation, if he felt they were ready for greater challenges he would move them up a grade, which then got them freshly motivated.

One of the best things about home schooling, according to Star, is that, "We can go travelling whenever we wish and just bring our schooling along. And it sure makes the miles go by!" Asked what she thinks is the main advantage, she says, "Home schooling gave me the chance to learn and study about other things, especially our religion, culture and outdoor living. Also, by using weekends to catch up, I can go to ceremonies or even spend the day snowboarding anytime during the week, when others are in school."

Okan never attended a class of public school, but a couple of the kids have spent time with friends and cousins whose teachers gave permission. Star says she's liked these experiences and sometimes back home afterwards has yearned for the social life they offered, but she assures me it's never been an important issue and that it really doesn't matter to her now, at all.

She was surprised at how much classroom time was spent "fooling around," talking, making jokes, annoying the teacher. She said it seemed they only learned a little bit about one subject, then class was over and they went on to something else, whereas here at home she spends a long time on a subject before moving on. She'd been somewhat shy to go, in part because the girls of her age were mostly in higher grades, but she was relieved to find that most of what they were studying had already been covered in her correspondence courses. She noticed overall that they weren't doing anything she didn't understand.

The least popular subject here at home has been math, which the kids say is mainly because of the way their correspondence courses presented it. Some clever sages decreed that a thing called "new math" was to be stressed, though the main stress seemed to be on us. When mama-teacher couldn't figure out the instructions she sent for papa-principal, who couldn't either, perhaps using that occasion to finally admit that math was his worst subject all through school. In the end, Beverly brought a tutor out here several times, until the boys caught on good enough to keep going.

"The real heck of it," says Okan now, "is that we've never used any of that so-called new math since, and I can't imagine when we would. Instead, I don't feel I'm so good at ordinary everyday math which I think the schooling should have emphasized. "Star has recently been having difficulties with it, so Okan tried cheering her up by saying, "You have to take 12 years of math no matter what, so they need to find something to fill in the blank spaces in between; find new ways to confuse you."

As Okan and Star approach the time to start their own families, they both say they'd like to home school their kids "if circumstances allow." Based on their experiences they figure to put major emphasis on discipline, being strict about getting a certain amount of work done each day. They figure they'd allow their kids a lot of freedom otherwise, so they could talk and visit in between school work, read magazines and play their radios, get up and move around, so long as the agreed-upon amount gets done by the end of each day. Okan adds that he would offer bonuses as incentives, but Star's not so sure if that's a good idea.

Starting in the middle grades, Beverly actually tried offering the incentive of small cash payments for completed course papers, but they still balked; this was mainly the two middle boys, who have always preferred the outdoors to studying at desks.

Home schooling in our old cabin, with Beverly teaching the boys from books, while I work on a book of my own at the desk in the background.
Brian Clarkson Photo

20.
A Tree Full of Eagles

Some of the best amusement park rides take you on boats through waters lined with surprises and adventures, and I've enjoyed my share of those. But I didn't count on getting a lifetime pass to such a ride with my purchase of this land. I don't even have to stand in line to get aboard, though somebody has to come pick me up at the bridge ten miles downstream afterwards, or else bring me about the same distance upstream to start with. Either way, we're about half way in the middle of a long stretch that lets me float at a gentle speed for two or three hours through total wilderness. The only exception are the Canadian Pacific Railway tracks that run more or less parallel, meaning that I usually exchange friendly greetings with a train crew or two.

Coming down this river for the first time was quite a revelation since we'd already lived on its shores for a number of years. We discovered a whole new world all around us, seemingly unexplored. It was in the month of March, just as winter was changing to spring. The water and air were still cold, with patches of snow and ice here and there, but also with the water level at its lowest point and thus least dangerous. In fact it was so low that we had to pole ourselves off several gravel bars wherever the river was too wide and shallow.

The trip got off to a memorable start as we rounded the first bend and floated silently right up to a thickly furred bush wolf standing unaware on an icy ledge at the riverbank, turned the other way. A look of tremendous fear was reflected from the poor creature's eyes when he finally noticed us, as though he expected to be blown to bits in the next instant. He may have seen friends and relatives to whom this happened, since the common response among people with guns in this region is to shoot coyotes and wolves on sight. He suddenly took off like a teenager at the wheel of a hot rod, taking several short slippery bounds before he got a good grip on the ice, then running at top speed towards the nearest forest cover, while we continued floating on out of sight.

Coming around a sharp bend just a few miles above our homestead, we interrupted a strange wilderness feast. Lying dead and half submerged in a pool of water under a cut bank was a big cow elk that had probably broken through the thin ice and drowned. Sitting in the bare branches of a single tall cottonwood tree right on shore was a flock of large birds, all of which turned out to be eagles. Without paddling, talking or making any other movements except to turn our heads, we drifted by this tree and counted a total of 18, all sitting in silence and staring back at us as we passed. That was a very eerie experience. They were bald eagles, most of them mature birds with white tails and heads, though there were also a few brownish, black speckled young ones. They are hunters of fish and eaters of carrion; whenever we have a successful hunt we watch the place where we leave the entrails, for bald eagles will usually be among the first scavengers coming down to check them out. One time I returned to the carcass of an elk I'd shot, after a couple hours of absence, spooking up a "white head" (as they are called in Blackfoot) whose head and tail were actually bright pink. This eagle had gotten right into the bloody body that I'd left opened up on the ground. The heart and liver were torn apart and spoiled, though the rest of the meat was untouched.

We had only one mishap on that first canoe trip, but it was enough to give us a taste of possible dangers, especially in higher and faster waters. At one of the many places where the main river narrowed into a fast and deep channel, it also made a sharp left bend. We had the place sized up from a distance as we headed into it, but noticed too late that a dead tree lay partly submerged, right in the midst of that tight bend. We tried hard to paddle away from it, but the water's force was far too strong, sucking us right towards that tree and in an instant turning us sideways up against it, whereupon the water pulled it over and filled it.

All three of us got thrown into the icy current, though somehow we were able to stay on our feet and hold on to our paddles.

Ten year old Wolf was my main concern, but in short order we managed to grab the canoe, our food and other things, then we dragged ourselves safely up on shore, where we soon had a fire going to dry everything out. With high water, later in spring, such capsizing could be fatal, since it would be hard to get back out of the raging currents. At such times the river can run several feet deep and nearly half a mile across.

Beverly and I setting out on another
adventurous ride down the river near our home.

21.

The Crazy Apple Bear

There are always bears roaming near our homestead, so it's
hard not to encounter them. People often don't realize how their
activities affect wild animals, bears being among the most suscep-
tible. For instance, I had never gone around our homestead looking at it from a bear's point of view, or I'd have cleaned up our
act much earlier.

For a start, there was the dog food. Having little room in the
family cabin for 50 pound sacks, I usually dumped the contents
into a metal trash can, put on the lid, and left it sitting beside the
dog dish, out in the woodshed behind the house. We were sort of
in between good guard dogs at this time; the two we had right
then were some sort of little short-haired, small bodied mongrel
variety that well-meaning relatives on the reserve gave to us after
hearing that our last dog had died. These two were beyond the
age of easy training, yet they had learned nothing worthwhile,
seemingly not even the ordinary dog wisdom. They kind of
bumbled around here, barked endlessly at every darn thing, yet
were so friendly and eager to please that I hesitated getting rid of
them.

We were gone for a few days, visiting relatives and attending
ceremonies over on the prairie, where these dogs had come from.
I filled their pail with far more food than they'd need while we
were gone, then poured a full bucket of fresh water. When we
came back, only the smarter of the two came out to greet us; we
never saw the other one again, though the kids later found its tail
nearby. In the woodshed, all the dog food was gone, including
what I'd stored in the trash can, which was on its side, empty and
somewhat beat up. At the back of the woodshed were the culprit's
"fingerprints," or claw marks, where a big bear had first tried to
tear off some boards to get at the food, before he found that the
front of the woodshed was open. Whether the dumb dog was an

hor d'ourve or a dessert we couldn't tell, but it had been a chubby thing and there was no sign of it, so we guessed that Mr. Bruin gulped it down and made his own dog chow.

Sure enough, the same night just before dark that old bear showed up and started snooping around in our yard again. He was a big black one, at least up to my waist on his four feet. The remaining dog said nothing and was nowhere to be seen. It quickly became apparent that he'd been so frightened that he wouldn't even bark anymore. Finally I went out with my shotgun and fired a round into the air over the bear's head, which caused him to run off pretty fast. I came back into the house feeling satisfied, since usually when a wild animal gets scared with a gun like that they take the hint and go away. But not this one!

Some of our bulk food was stored in bins and boxes over at a little guest cabin, which sat otherwise closed up and empty about a hundred feet from the house. The next night that bear was back, checking to see if he could gain entry into this other place. He obviously smelled the grub inside, trying to get at it by tearing off boards as if he were a wrecker with a crowbar. It was dark, so I took a flashlight along with the shotgun and went to chase him away. Again I fired over his head, and again he took off, but not so far this time. I had no sooner gone back into the house and gotten settled when I again heard sounds of destruction in the darkness of the night. He must have kept one ear bent my way, for I stepped out very quietly yet he heard me and took off before I could see him or fire another shot.

For the next couple of weeks this bear pretty well took over our lives. He didn't show up every single night, which made it all the worse. Now, at the same time we were also having the usual fall migration of mice, who were looking for winter food and a home. When you're trying to sleep, a mouse running on the other side of a nearby wall can sound an awful lot like a bear trying to get into further mischief. I don't know how many times I jumped up during the nights, gun and flashlight firmly in my hand, heart pounding loudly in the silent darkness, before I realized that the racket I'd heard was just another little squeaky thing with a long tail.

Windy nights were even worse for bothersome noises, and winds often blow through here in the river bottom and across our meadow. Bushes and grasses scraping up against the house, or a tree trunk groaning nearby, would get me up and armed right away. I'd stand silently, holding my breath and listening. I couldn't just plain wait up for the bear because I never knew when he was coming; as a result, I thought every sound was him. I think my ears almost grew bigger during those weeks, dreading to hear his next arrival.

One night loud noises woke me up just in time to hear that same bear bump solidly into a big wagon wheel that we had leaning against the front of our house for a decoration. I jumped up and looked out through a side window, seeing his dark shape ambling past in the dim moonlight. Beverly awoke and asked what was up, so I told her to open the curtain and look out the back window by our bed to see where he was going. Still half asleep, she rolled over on her pillow, raised up on one elbow, flung the curtain back, only to look directly into that bear's big black face, less than a foot away. He was holding his paws to the window at the same time, trying to look in. The former Miss Little Bear (her maiden name) screamed at the current Mr. Big Bear, causing him to drop down with fright and run off. It was sure the end of him for that night, but it was for Beverly too, as I recall.

In those days her parents still liked to travel regularly and visit far from their reserve home, including an annual trip to their good friend Donny Sampson of the Yakima tribe, down in the state of Washington. Donny was widely known not only as a champion pow-wow dancer, but also as a successful farmer among the people of his tribe. The in-laws always came back from his place with their truck loaded down with fresh fruit and produce, some of which they usually dropped off for us.

That fall we received our supply from Yakima during the weeks that this big bear was bothering us, though he didn't come by to say hello to the elderly couple who share his name. We put the food that they gave us into solid boxes on the front porch of our house, figuring the wild fellow wouldn't be so daring as to come inside. Besides the food, we also had on that porch a little border collie pup whose mother was said to have been an excellent family guard. Because of a white spot on its black tail we named this dog Tippy. With trouble cruising the landscape at night, we kept the little newcomer on the porch for safety.

Well, this bear was more daring than I thought; in fact, he was beginning to get downright dangerous. On his first attempt, he managed to knock one of that room's big windows right out of its frame, though I must confess to having done a poor job at nailing it in. Luckily the glass pane landed on a pile of new gunnysacks we'd just received, so nothing broke. But there was a loud bang when it fell, scaring the bear off. I went outside and tacked the window back into its frame, then nailed a sturdy board across it from the outside. An hour later the bear woke me up as he pulled on that board, determined to make his way back in. There was a loud crack, then again the sound of the window falling out without breaking. I grabbed my flashlight and shotgun on the way up to the front of the house, Beverly hot on my trail, though for some reason our three little boys remained asleep through all this.

Looking from the kitchen window into that front room with a flashlight instantly revealed the big black hulk of that bear, busily rummaging for the fresh produce that he could readily smell in the damp night air. Beverly panicked and shouted, "Shoot him through the window, quick!" I told her I couldn't do that, since there was only a thin door between him and us. If I shot and only wounded him he might be just as likely to come through here as to go back out the window. With sleeping kids nearby, I didn't want a wounded bear in the house! Cold sweat broke out on my forehead and my heart beat fast while I stood and aimed the shotgun at the door trying to decide what to do next.

The waving flashlight and our excited talk was apparently too much for the intruder, as he jumped back out through the empty window and took off into the dark. Our first concern was for Tippy, who hadn't made a sound. Her mother might have been a good watchdog, but the pup was still too young. I was hoping she hadn't been hurt. I opened the door and shined the light around, but there was no sign of the little creature. We went over to the open window and stood in the dark listening silently to hear which way the bear had gone. Suddenly there was a short, high-pitched yelp, the sort that a dog makes when you step on it. It was our pup, I was sure, and it seemed as though that mean bear had snapped its neck. He was probably eating it up right then, I thought, though I dared not jump out into the dark and go after him. At that point this particular bear became an outlaw, an enemy of our family and an intruder into our home. I knew I would have to shoot him if we were ever to find peace again.

We were still standing in shock and some fear when we heard a tiny thumping sound behind us in the dark. We both jumped with a start and turned around, my flashlight revealing movement among a bunch of those gunny sacks over in the far corner. Closer inspection found little Tippy underneath them, her nose towards the wall, her tail beating a pitiful message that she'd really appreciate friendship. I picked her up and gave her a big hug, which made the tail beat much faster, though she was shivering as if it was in the middle of winter. I was just about to say some words of comfort when Beverly interrupted my thoughts by shouting, "He's back!"

When I turned to see who she meant, there was the bear again, looking right through that same knocked out window just behind us, less than five feet away. I dropped the pup and jumped up with my gun, but that big black form just quietly melted back into the night. Damn, I was starting to get mad! That is, when I wasn't getting my pants scared off. He was a formidable enemy and so far he was getting the best of me.

But now I'd had enough, so I lay awake and waited, knowing that he had himself worked up enough to come back for another try. I'd already opened the window next to the one he was using, so when I heard him outside again I just quietly stuck the shotgun out into his direction and let go of a round of buckshot. There was no sound from him, nor did he ever come back after that to bother us again. Needless to say, he was the cause of many more fast heartbeats during the next few nights, at least until the snows of winter assured me that he was gone for good.

Byron Harmon Photo

22.

Mean Mama Bear and Meaner Mama Dog

One day, years later, we had a three-way encounter among three different families that turned out pretty good, but could have quickly become dangerous. I was typing in my caboose when I heard the dogs scramble out from their favorite place down betwen the railroad ties, where it was nice and shady. Moments later I heard them running fast and barking ferociously, so I went out to see the cause. In the distance I caught a glimpse of my boys heading down hurriedly from the house on their bicycles. They had been outside when the dogs first took off and knew that this particular bark meant something unusual was actually in sight.

Baby and Boss were then about three and just getting into their prime, so they were far ahead, with the more elderly Tippy trailing. About the time I passed her on my bike, the other two changed their barking style to indicate they now had something at bay. They were at the edge of a thick stand of young green-leaved poplars, about forty feet ahead, at the foot of a slope leading up to a pine covered hill. Suddenly a good sized bear stood up from among those poplars, looking pretty big and mad, while behind her, two cubs went scampering up a couple of trees. Not only had we chased a mad mama bear, but she had a yellowish coat like a grizzly, not the black we normally see around here. The two young dogs spun around and took off in the opposite direction the moment they saw her. Thus they passed me, heading home, while at about the same time their mother seemed more determined than ever to get at whatever was in our territory that had so scared her kids.

Tippy didn't hesitate for a moment, even when she finally saw that the target was a big bear. The bruin, in turn, realized that *this* dog meant business, *and* that it was her home ground, so she joined her cubs up another one of those thin poplars, while Tippy stood underneath barking. By then the boys had arrived on their bikes, so Tippy finally left the tree and came over to join us, fully out of breath, wagging her tail excitedly, looking proud as can be. It turned out to be a cinnamon colored variation of a black bear, of which we've seen a couple more since. We watched from a distance as she slowly climbed back down, then coaxed her cubs into leaving with her for quieter places.

Here's how Beverly recalls another bear encounter: "The kids and I were home alone, with me still getting used to this forest life and the many wild animals. Suddenly Wolf came running into the house calling, 'Mom, there's a bear playing on my swing.'

"So I grabbed the shotgun from over the door, then went out and fired a round into the air, thinking to scare it away. But that darned bear just continued to play with the kids' swing, although it did look up into the pine branches for a few moments to see where all the needles were dropping down from.

"At that point Wolf, who was only four years old, looked at me and said with disgust, 'Mom, that's not how you do it; *this* is how!'" Without further ado he ran towards that bear, screaming at the top of his voice, though we were less than twenty feet apart. The next thing I saw was a big black ball of fur speeding off towards the distant woods."

Byron Harmon Photo

23.

Missed His Flight South

It was an auspicious day for me, trying to get the final work done on our new studio, moving the bedding, typewriter and other things over here from my old caboose, which had served as an office for the previous ten years. I spent the early afternoon varnishing the last of our wooden window frames, while the sun barely warmed up the air. It was early November and the previous night we'd had the season's first snowfall, so I considered it the start of winter, calendar dates not withstanding.

Suddenly I was startled by a white bird circling down from out of the blue, windless sky, landing just 15 or 20 feet from me. What in the world, I thought to myself, having never seen one of these. It looked like a little white crane, with skinny black legs, a longish neck and a thick bill. But it was way too small to be a Sandhill Crane, the only kind that regularly come around here.

What piqued my curiosity right from the start was why, with all this vast wilderness around, did this strange bird decide to land so near to me? There are always things we can learn from nature, so I often watch for meanings in the actions of birds and animals. The spiritual culture we've inherited from some of our familiy elders encourage us to observe unusual events in nature, and includes songs and ceremonies whereby we honor them. In that regard, I considered the fact of a strange white bird sitting so nearby in the cold white snow as something significant.

For the first minutes it stood quite still, then started to bob its head around, looking this way and that, very regal, even kind of cute. After that it started walking, very slowly and decisively. In fact, stalking would perhaps be a better description, as if searching for something lost on the snow covered ground. I was in a rush to complete the varnishing work, yet I figured any moment this unusual bird would fly away and I'd never see one like it again, so I kept my eyes on its every move.

But it stayed, so eventually I went back to finish my work on the windows, then got ready to haul more stuff over from the caboose. Could it have read my mind? I doubt it, but by the time I had my hands cleaned and the brush put away, that white bird had already walked over to my caboose ahead of me, standing at the bottom of its steps like some kind of little butler.

It moved away a few feet when I finally got over there myself, but otherwise it didn't seem to mind my coming. I then got a load of stuff and hauled it over to the studio. By the time I had it unpacked the bird was halfway over too, following the same trail I used through the snow. The dogs had come down from the old house, meanwhile, and were laying outside the studio door, so I cautioned them about getting any thoughts to chase that bird, after which they pretended not to even see it, though it walked within 15 feet of them.

A while later the bird again headed over to my caboose, its visit seeming more and more strange. I halfway expected it to start talking to me next, or to let me know that it had lived with humans. I mean, we have other friendly birds here - one or two even learned to take bread crumbs from our hands - but nothing ever acted like this except our family dogs, and to a lesser extent our cats. But a wild bird?

I finally went up to the house to tell Star and Beverly, so they came back with me to bear witness. At first Beverly was kind of spooked by the story and said I should shoot the bird. Some of her old people thought that a bird hanging around a person was the bringer of death, but I refused to shoot the messenger, seeing nothing that I considered evil; it was even dressed in white. However, as if to test our resolve, the strange bird took off before our very eyes and flew at a low level down to the old family house, landing in one of the pine trees right out front.

From that tree it then barely cleared the roof of the house as it sailed over to the adjacent chicken coop and settled on its roof for a spell. But soon it flew back down directly to the new studio as if specifically to join us. For the rest of the afternoon, wherever I went the white bird eventually followed. Now and then it would stop and tense up, then jab its beak down among the thick grass, coming up with some kind of tidbit that it tossed around a few times on its beak before it got swallowed. Occasionally it apparently got a bad deal, as it tossed the item away, but the rest it ate. Only once was I able to see what it caught, a big, struggling grasshopper, which it swallowed. Food was not its problem, but the bird was otherwise definitely out of its element.

Cattle egret, said my bird book later, some three or four thousand miles from its home (which is mainly in the Southeast U.S.). I last saw it just before dark, flying up into the trees behind the new studio. By the next morning it was gone. I've often wondered if this poor bird ever found its way out of that snowstorm and back across the North American continent to its nice warm home range.

O.H.W.

24.

The Deer That Signifed Death

Willie Eagle Plume was a noted tribal elder, singer, storyteller, medicine man, and plain old nice guy. He was born in 1903, called in the Blackfoot language "The Year the Mountain Fell Down," referring to a famous disaster in the Crowsnest Pass region, when the face of Turtle Mountain slid down over the sleeping town of Frank, Alberta and snuffed out a number of lives. We drove by this place each time we brought him over from the reserve to visit with us, and he always stared at the carpet of boulders in silence.

During the few years that we were together, Willie and I grew very fond of each other. It helped that he was Beverly's dad's uncle, a favorite member of the family, and a man eager to relive some of the tribal traditions he grew up with as a boy. We met when Beverly and I first got together and liked each other right away. Since I already had long hair and wore it in braids, he decided to join me, having worn braids himself a few times in his earlier years. I always called him by his Indian name Atsitsina, which means Prairie Owl Man, while he in turn addressed me by his own father's name Natosina, or Sun Man, the name he passed on to me when I joined the family. Old Natosina's wife - Atsitsina's mother - was named Sikskiaki, or Black Faced Woman, a name inherited by Beverly shortly after her birth.

Willie Eagle Plume was an outdoorsman all his life, living along the Blood Reserve's Bullhorn River with his dad, brothers, and their families. He loved to tell his father's tales about the old time outdoor life of buffalo hunting, existing with nothing but fur robes for warmth and hide tipis for shelter. He understood the reason I brought my family out here to live in the wilds, and he seemed to understand what I meant about that "ancestral ember" glowing deep in my heart. Willie and I took sweatbaths together, went for walks here in the mountains, and attended Sun

Dance camps and other ceremonies on the prairies. One summer I even took him to New York City on his only airplane flight, then on to Washington, DC, where we spent ten days as guests of the Smithsonian Institute, demonstrating traditional crafts at their annual Folklife Festival. It was the trip of his lifetime.

Willie Eagle Plume hadn't been much of a hunter - especially not when compared to his dad - preferring to raise cattle and getting his substitute buffalo meat that way. But he liked hearing about my hunting and outdoor adventures and he enjoyed getting to eat some of the elk and deer meat that I brought. Unusual incidents involving animals were always of special interest to him, so I looked forward to telling him about a particular odd incident I had with a deer one winter day.

Hunting season had long been over, so I was checking my territory on snowshoes without a gun, just going around visiting my animal neighbors. By the time I got to the base of our nearby cliffs I'd already seen a couple herds of elk and some whitetail deer. The snow was deep and firm in the cooler places, where I tried to walk, but the more open and exposed areas had thawed and then frozen a few times, so now they were slippery and treacherous.

Suddenly a big deer burst out of the trees just ahead of me, running straight uphill into the cliffs, as they generally do when spooked. I slogged forward as fast as I could in order to reach a small clearing where I could sit down on a stump and watch this deer for a long ways. I've learned to know some of the better viewing places along my various trails and I always hope to see animals there in order to observe them.

This deer bounded along quite easily for a while, its big white tail floating gently in the air, the sounds of cracking snow bouncing off the stony walls further up and thus making a lot of racket. Then, without warning, the deer hit an exceptionally icy patch just where its steep uphill trail crested a rocky outcropping. By this time my own adrenalin was running, so I used my empty hands to pretend I was hunting this deer, getting off a moving shot just as it reached that same rocky crest and slick ice. For an instant it seemed to hang in mid air without coming back down, then it did sort of a somersault and disappeared on the far side of the outcropping, an area that I couldn't see from my viewpoint.

Still excited, I jumped up and moved over as quick as my snowshoes let me go, wanting to see how and where this deer would land. For sure it would be injured by such a fall, and perhaps I'd be of some help. But I couldn't see anything of it, no matter how hard I looked; there was only that rock outcropping, standing there silently.

I decided to go up and take a closer look, though I'd been on that steep cliff in similarly icy conditions before and swore I wouldn't do it again. Besides the slipperiness, there are boulders and big chunks of shale everywhere just waiting to break some bones. That is, if one of those big rocks overhead doesn't happen to crash down first and wipe you out.

The deer had been bedded down when I approached and was likely a buck without horns, since it was travelling alone. Probably an old buck too, from the size of it and its tracks. The bounds it took through the snow were so long that I could slide my snowshoes forward several times between them. When I reached the icy part I took my snowshoes off, since they'd make the steep climb even more dangerous, perhaps even impossible. As it was, I had on my high top moccasins of thick sheepskin, lovingly made by my wife, comfortable and warm on snowshoes; but the smooth leather soles gave me little grip on the ice. I knew that following this deer up the rocky slope was going to be no picnic. Using the various rocks and small trees as steps, I went along, sometimes crawling on my belly, dragging myself to the next step with my fingertips. Being dressed warm for the cool forests, I was soon perspiring from the open sunshine and exertion, but eventually I managed to reach that rocky outcropping.

There was one final sign of that deer, a foot-long scrape where one of its hooves had come down but found no solid grip, then after that, nothing! Not another sign anywhere, up or down. The bright sun was showing shadows on every break of the icy surface, so the deer's tracks should have been clearly visible, but there just didn't seem to be any. I could see the tracks coming up this far pretty easily, so where had it gone?

It was nearly straight down for over a hundred feet on the other side of the outcrop, the area that I hadn't been able to watch from below. If the deer had managed to catapult that far without touching ground it would have broken its neck, or at least been severely injured. I made a painstaking return, climbing back down the way I came, then combed the foot of that slope back and forth several times in vain, looking for any sign of that deer, either dead or showing that it had gotten away. It seemed unreal, but try as I might there just wasn't a trace to follow. I don't consider myself superstitious, but I have to admit to feeling very strange while going away from there. I've since gone back many times, but to this day I have no rational explanation for the disappearance of that deer.

Now, it so happened that I was going into town that afternoon anyway, so I decided to stop by and visit Andrew Michel, the old hunter and outdoorsman. When I finished telling him my story he didn't hesitate a moment, squinting hard into my eyes, saying almost angrily: "Well, now you're gonna lose somebody close to you - some old man!" I wondered if he meant himself, but that's all he would tell me, nor would he explain upon what he had based his statement. It was just a brief visit - we had other ones that were longer and in greater depth. But this one left me more unsettled than before.

The next day at mid-morning Beverly's dad showed up with another relative, having walked in through the snow three miles from the highway, since their car didn't have four-wheeled drive. When he got to the house and started crying we knew something was seriously wrong. It turned out that the previous morning, about the time I was involved with that deer on the ice, Willie Eagle Plume had put his head down on his youngest boy's shoulder and died of a heart attack. Since then I've often wondered what forces of nature got together so that I could witness such a strange event, then get such a grim interpretation, ending with the loss of my best old friend. It was an impressive way for an impressive man to step out of my life.

25.

The Hawk Between the Doors

It's tempting for kids living outdoors to want a wild animal for a pet, although we were pretty lucky here in getting to do without them except for one who came to us kind of accidentally. This was Iniskim's experience, so I'll let him tell it.

"I was about 12, when I decided one time to have a look inside of Okan's caboose. It's strange how I felt drawn to do that, since normally I didn't go in there for months. Inside I heard a scratching sound at the far end, so I went back to see what it was. At first I couldn't find anything, but then I heard the sound again and realized it was coming from a narrow space between two doors that were tied together to keep the caboose closed up. Looking down between them I could see a sparrow hawk with his wings outstretched, seeming pretty scared. Somehow he must have landed by those two doors and then slipped down in between them, but there wasn't enough room for him to fly back out. From the white splatters around him he'd already been there a couple of days and probably wouldn't have lasted much longer.

"Since I couldn't reach the hawk with my hands, I raced back to the house for our fishing net, which made it easy to pull him out. Then I took him home and built a quick cage with chicken wire, tall enough and long enough so he could fly between the branches that I put in there. With my .22 rifle I shot gophers and squirrels, and in that way he got back his strength and I got to spend time with a pretty bird.

"Once Okan and I were in the house when we heard weird screeching and hissing noises, so we ran back to investigate. Turns out our household cat had forced her way into the cage to get at the latest squirrel, which the hawk hadn't yet eaten. He didn't take to the cat's visit too kindly, being backed up on his perch as far as he could go, one leg up and a clawed foot facing forward like some karate champ, all the while screeching and hissing to let that cat know he didn't want it closer. For its part, the cat looked pretty leery too, trying to eat that gopher while staying on guard for an attack, since she couldn't make her way back out of the cage the way she got in. She rushed out the moment I opened that door, never trying that trick again.

"You told me right from the start that I couldn't keep this hawk, and you always told us that we shouldn't try to catch wild animals, but I kind of figured this one was sent to me and I saved its life, so I was looking forward to having it around for a while. But one day I was careless when I brought it outside of the cage, thinking I could trust its friendship and teach it to come back to me. Somehow it slipped out of my grasp and flew up on top of its cage, then it tried again and flew to the nearest tree branch, from where it looked back at me once more as if to say, "Looks like I'm really free," and it flew away for good.

"I'm glad I had this chance to be around a wild hawk for a while, to get food for it and watch how it eats. But I also realized from this experience how much nicer it is to just see these birds out on their own, not in a fenced enclosure."

Beverly's mom used to have a badger for a pet when she was young. It slept right in bed with her, being very smart and friendly. We have badgers around here and the kids talked a few times about repeating grandma's experience, but thankfully it never happened. Iniskim did have a ferret for a while, but that wasn't an animal from the wild, though in the end its half wild rambunctiousness caused Iniskim to give it back. It was constantly getting into things and running underfoot. Several times it was nearly crushed, and we always had to watch out that it didn't run out when we opened a door, since it would not have survived outdoors by itself.

We've also had this ferret's wild weasel cousins in our house a few times, and they sure are a mighty terror for their tiny size. Each time they came in specifically to get at deer meat that we had hanging up in a cool room. They didn't hesitate to attack a whole deer quarter, even to try dragging it away, though the meat was more than ten times their size. But there was no chance of catching one of these underfoot, the fastest moving thing I've ever witnessed inside our house, literally flashing from one spot to the next as we tried to throw them out. And fierce too, not hesitating to attack anything we used to try catching them with. No wonder the old Blackfeet considered this one of the most admirable animals, its black tipped, white winter pelts having about the same significance on traditional Blackfoot clothing as black and white eagle feathers have for people of other tribes.

26.

Leave it to Beavers

Dipping the ends of my paddle into the water quietly, I measured each stroke carefully to make the least disturbance while approaching the smallest of three beaver houses scattered along a two mile stretch of barely moving backwaters near our home. Finally I stopped paddling altogether, letting the momentum keep me drifting, tilting my body just slightly left and right to keep the boat on course. Suddenly I noticed a dark spot breaking the water about 100 feet ahead, moving steadily towards me. It had to be a beaver, though all I saw was the head and not its body or tail; we were on a collision course.

With bated breath I watched it get closer, until I could see clearly that it was indeed a beaver, a fairly big one. Not only that, but there were two tiny beavers clinging to it, which I'd never seen before. Mama beaver had taken her babies out for a swim on this warm spring afternoon, thus presenting me with a most memorable sight. She didn't notice my presence until we were just a few feet apart, at which point she slapped her tail loudly, spun over in a burst of energy and spray of water, then dived down into her nearby house, all within just a couple of seconds. Strange to say, those little ones held on as tight as if they were kids going through the corkscrew on a roller coaster ride.

Later I came back by that same beaver house on my way home, again drifting up silently until I was within inches of the bank into which the main chamber had been built. At that point I stuck the paddle straight down into the soft grey-blue mud and held on tight, thereby becoming firmly anchored. Then I heard sounds from within, whimpering sounds like those made by human babies being changed and fed, sounds of love perhaps, and of satisfaction. Except for the wall of mud and sticks between us, we were within touching distance of each other. That was certainly a moment of life in harmony with nature.

Maybe it was the romantic connection to the Wild West that first brought out my fondness for all things beaver (though not for the trapping part of it). Like buffalo, though not driven quite so close to extinction, beavers are animals linked with humankind and the frontiers of nature. An especially admirable animal, even with its strange tail, perhaps easier for us humans to relate to than buffalo because of the clever way they build big family homes and stock them with seasonal food supplies.

That back channel didn't have any beavers living in it when we first moved here, and the way they finally came was sort of mysterious. Of three beaver lodges, only one was here then, laying scattered and destroyed at the bottom of the channel after some vicious logger on strike at a nearby mill came out here for "quick bucks," using a stick of dynamite to blow up the beaver house and its occupants, though it was said that he didn't find enough beaver pelt afterwards to sell. Since our area has plenty of willows and young poplars that beavers like to eat, I wondered if there was anything I could do to make them move back in. I went to see the local fish and wildlife department, where a sympathetic fellow phoned a local trapper who said he'd be glad to catch a couple of beavers for me with live traps and help me get them to our channel.

For a short while the idea of transporting beavers sounded intriguing; after all, they do it with fish. But then I began to wonder if this was the right thing, or was I imposing my will on nature too much? A couple of miles from here runs the main Kootenay River channel and there are always beavers going up and down it, as evidenced by the shiny remains of freshly chewed wood. If our back channel was right for them, surely they'd find their own way here, as animals have always done. The trapper said the same thing in a different way when he warned me, "I'll bring you a couple of live beavers, no problem, but I can't guarantee they'll stay." No use going through all that hassle just to put a couple more into the river traffic, I finally decided.

Ten or twelve years went by with no immigrant beavers taking up residence near us. Oh, they'd come up into the channel now and then, leaving their calling cards of chewed sticks behind - a few times from our canoe we even saw them swimming. But there were no houses and dams that would signify an actual settlement. Mind you, with all the other wild animals close to our house it wasn't necessary that we have beavers too, but I always kept a special lookout for any signs of them.

Then our family took an important step within the tribal culture and religion that we practice. We had learned that a humble old man named Mike Swims Under was the one single elder still living in the Blackfoot Confederacy who could teach us the ancient beaver medicine dance and ceremony, which was thought to have been lost a couple of generations ago. Because of my fondness for beavers, we had accumulated some of the articles needed in that ceremony and were thrilled to find someone who could teach us what to do with them.

Mike stayed here with us for a week, admitting that he was a bit rusty on the subject, though he'd been born and raised with it by his parents. He never expected to help revive this ceremony in his old age, any more than we had expected to find someone who could do so. This is a complex topic that is hard to describe in written words (though it's been tried, and it probably will be again); besides, the ritual itself is not the point of this story.

To our amazement, the day after I returned from taking Mike Swims Under back to his Montana reservation home, there were fresh signs of beavers around that old blown-up beaverhouse. I saw it from a distance while paddling along quietly - fresh willow sticks, yellow against the bluish waters, conspicuous when compared to the bleached look of those from the past. Nearby I discovered what turned out to be the first layer of a new beaver dam, which meant the beavers were settling in. That dam has since been expanded to about four feet high, stretching some 50 feet across our back channel. The old house has a new one built over it, with a main chamber up against the bank, same as that smallest one I saw the mother beaver dive into later on with her kits. In the ten years since then, a third house has been built further down the channel, a freestanding one, out in the middle of the water. It is now also the biggest of the three, reaching a height of nearly 15 feet from its base.

For a couple of years all three houses were occupied by beaver families. During that time I saw beavers whenever I went near the water. In fact, they "logged" our area much like the local mechanized crews do when they reach a new forest. And I regret to admit that those beavers are darned near as wasteful. For instance, a few hundred feet from our new studio there's a neat little stand of poplar trees whose leaves turn yellow every fall and look really pretty, with green pines growing all around them. The stand was made up of about 30 mature poplars, maybe 20 to 30 inches around at their bases. Not huge trees by any means, but they've grown for many years and couldn't quickly be replaced. One day an especially ambitious couple of beavers discovered this grove along the edge of our field. We happened to be gone at a pow-wow for the weekend, and beavers can sure work fast when they want to. By the time we got back home and realized what they were up to, half the grove was already down, each pointed stump glistening brightly in the sun. "Leave it to Beaver," I thought unhappily to myself. I hesitated making any response, since I don't like to interfere with nature's processes, especially not when one of my favorite animals is involved. But the darned rascals were ruining a rare piece of my scenery!

He who hesitates is lost, alright - those buck-toothed critters continued working every night. One time I was standing outside and actually heard one of my beloved poplars go crashing down. Finally I could take no more, so I dug out a roll of chicken wire left from Star's hen run and wrapped pieces of this around the bottom of each remaining tree's trunk. Ironically, a heat wave soon after this made water levels drop, so that the channel next to this grove went dry, thus the beavers quit coming to it altogether. Which brings up the worst and most wasteful part of this story. Except for some branches that they ate during the course of their work, plus a couple of larger limbs that they chopped up and brought to the now dry channel, those beavers didn't do a thing with my beautiful trees, and it wasn't until several years later that I finally started sawing them up into sweat-lodge fire lengths.

More recently, only the biggest of the three beaver houses has been in use regularly, though the other two get temporay occupants now and then. When these two are still empty by late fall, muskrats invariably move in. It's easy to tell which residents are there: beavers leave willow sticks; muskrats leave only reeds and slough grasses. One or the other of these is usually found by the door of occupied houses..

In talking to the boys about the ten years since beavers began living almost in our backyard, we agreed that the experience has given us a much greater appreciation for the making of wildlife films and photographs, like ones that show beavers building their houses, chewing down trees, or even wrestling with each other. In all our years we've hardly seen any of these activites, not because we wouldn't like to, but because we just don't go out of our way to study our neighbors and see what they're up to.

The beaver's muskrat cousin is a critter we see a lot more of. They often let us get fairly close to them with our canoe, so we've been able to watch them building their mud and reed houses, playing in and near the water, even mating. Since muskrats reproduce more young than beavers, they live more crowded, and apparently they fight a lot. The few I trapped many years ago had their skins bruised all over from bites. One time in the middle of a recent winter I found a wounded one lying bloody in the snow, not far from its house, tracks showing that it had come out already in a bloody condition, presumably after getting a beating from someone tougher.

I watched a pair of muskrats mating one sunny day for about an hour. The excitement actually started about ten minutes before I saw this pair, as I was paddling back from an unsuccessful fishing trip to the river. Through a thick stand of reeds I looked ahead to see a big bull moose less than 100 yards at the other end of an open stretch of water. He was half submerged, his head having just come up with a mouthful of greenery. Water spilling from his mouth was apparently making more noise than me, since he hadn't noticed my presence. But he did notice my back-paddling, as I struggled to keep my boat from drifting any closer. At 75 yards he looked pretty formidable! All the more so since, by being in a boat, my position was pretty awkward. But he took off in the opposite direction, going at a fast trot through the

water, which was nearly as deep as his long legs. It was easy to
see why Beverly's forefathers named this animal "sikstisu," or
"black charging through the woods."

After that I came to the biggest of the three beaver houses, so I
slowed down my paddling to see if any occupants were about.
Sure enough, there were two distinct lines moving along through
the water just ahead of me, but when I got closer they turned out
to be muskrats instead of beavers. One seemed to be chasing the
other, very determinedly, but not in a hurried way. The one being chased made soft cooing sounds, so I realized she was a female being courted by a male, and that they were performing
their mating ritual. In typical female fashion (modern "liberated"
ideas notwithstanding) she let him get close, only to turn suddenly away and frustrate his advances, after which she cooed until he
tried again. It was hard not to think about comparisons and sym-
bolisms....

Mister Muskrat finally managed to mount his Missus, though
it was just for a quickie, done while they continued their swim.
They were so involved in all this that I drifted within ten or fifteen feet of them, yet they still didn't notice. At one point the female cooed, then got out on shore and waited until her paramour
had a quickie with her on dry land, after which they both went
back into the water. There she continued her cooing and evad-
ing, until at last she again submitted, very briefly.

These mating sessions alternated from water to shore for some
time in the pleasant sunshine, until suddenly a beaver came out
of its house to find out what was going on, nearly bumping into
my boat in the process. Slapping its tail loudly as a warning, the
beaver quickly dove back down. The result was similar to what
happens when a friend bangs on the bedroom door during a par-
ty, with the two muskrats instantly diving into the water and disappearing from sight. "The nerve of that man," I thought I heard
her saying on the way down.

27.

Romance of the Eagle

From the edge of our rocky cliffs I looked down about 1,500 feet into the valley floor and the winding river beyond, feeling the morning sun at my back and a warm breeze blowing into my face from the south. Suddenly a large shadow loomed from my right; by the time I turned towards it we were just inches apart. It was a golden eagle, a giant of a bird, its outstretched wings spanning five feet or more. It sailed past me in almost total silence, with only its countless black and white feathers making a soft whoosh! It never turned to look at me, though I'm sure it knew very well that I was there. Humans throughout the ages have honored this bird, this big silent sailor and hunter of the sky, going places and doing things that we can only dream about....

"The eagle is among the highest of living beings in our culture," an elderly Cree friend and medicine man named Ernest Tootoosis told me one time years ago, as he sat on the tailgate of his truck and slowly plucked the brown and white barred feathers from the large body of a recently-killed adult golden eagle. "The Indian gets power from the eagles; we recognize them as supreme; they bring our prayers to the Creator." Words to contemplate; perhaps words of wisdom, depending on your orientation; strange words coming from a man who had, that same morning, shot the eagle now lying in his lap.

"Sure, I know the law says it's not allowed to kill eagles," my friend proclaimed, "but that's a white man's law, and this is going to be used for Indian purposes. That law was forced upon our people, but no one can force me to give up my Indian faith. That's what this eagle represents, faith in the ways of my ancestors. It doesn't matter whether the feathers end up being used for prayers, for ceremonies, or for dancing at pow-wows."

When you look at Ernest's ways in the overall context of native cultural survival, it's hard to disagree with what he says. Seldom has the stereotype "American Indian" been represented in folk-lore and history without "his" feather bonnet, or some other way of wearing eagle feathers. The enthusiasm for this symbol has grown tremendously in recent years with the revival of native customs and dances. Pow-wow participation is greater than ever, with seemingly every costume aflutter with the feathers of eagles. It's a dazzling spectacle for dancers and viewers alike. They've also become popular on rearview mirrors, where they presumably provide inspiration, serving as sort of a symbol for native North America, much in the way that drivers of other nationalities identify themselves with flag decals or abbreviated letters indicating their country.

But there's a need for concern when you take away the romance and think of cold hard reality. Those countless feathers represent the lives of a great many birds, often-times shot, when other pressures are already threatening the eagle's existence around the world. Of course, a lot of feathers seen at pow-wows nowadays come from government offices, obtained from eagles that have died naturally or been accidentally killed on highways, railways, or by electric power lines.

"What about all the eagles, hawks, and so forth wiped out by poisons being sprayed all over the country by farmers, and by industries?" Ernest asked me. "What about the ones that are shot by sheep men who claim eagles are taking their lambs? Let the government solve all those problems first, before they come and ask us Indians not to kill eagles for our culture." Ernest was a man of integrity, using the eagle parts that he gathered with great care and respect. However, their scarcity has created a sizeable black market in the sale of eagle feathers, where no moral justification is used and the ritual becomes money.

"Twelve Indians indicted for trafficking in eagle feathers," says a recent headline about a lengthy undercover investigation by federal agents, both in Canada and the U.S. Those charged were said to have been part of an international network selling dead eagles simply for profit, feather by feather, or else turned into so-called "artifacts," which vastly increases the profits. Even in Indian country a choice black and white eagle tailfeather can bring $100 or more these days from a pow-wow dancer, or a tribal elder not wanting to wait for a government hand out.

Without a doubt the most enduring symbol of traditional native life in North America, the eagle is nevertheless surrounded by mystery that relatively few people understand, native or not. If an eagle lands near a reservation home where there is a gun, chances are good that someone will take a shot at it. This person will not usually care where the bird came from, or whether it might be a mother searching for food to bring back to her young. If confronted with such issues, the shooter might reply that it doesn't matter, using words such as "the eagle was given to the Indian" or, "I'm just following my heritage."

A study of flags, costumes and other cultural symbols from around the world will reveal that eagles are nearly everyone's "heritage;" they seem to be revered by most people, and weren't necessarily "given" to anyone. Furthermore, the traditional native process of obtaining eagle feathers involved a very serious ritual among most tribes, for which few persons ever qualified, and from which the resulting feathers were highly prized and appreciated. Those who then wore these feathers did so very sparingly, with each one representing a brave deed on the warpath, else a special ceremonial accomplishment. Few of us will ever have the honor to see eagles at home in their nests, or to watch them nearby for any length of time. Someday the chance for that may disappear altogether, especially if we don't speak out against abuses that eagles often go through in order to survive in the modern world. Those who feel strongly about what the eagle represents should also speak out most loudly for its protection, so that future generations can still look for them in the open skies.

28.

Winter Jay

From a note in my journal: "There's a blue Stellar's Jay that's been hanging out in the pine trees next to my caboose since the start of winter, yet it won't touch bread crumbs, apple cores, or any other things that I put out for it. This is the first one of its kind I've seen here in 11 years,. Strange to say, it seems to have decided to remain for the winter. Wish we could establish a friendship, since jays are among my favorite birds. They're talkative and sociable, hopping around without apparent fear of humans, yet always keeping one eye out just in case there's trouble..."

A couple of weeks later I wrote, "My bluejay friend is still here; it must have read what I said about bread crumbs though, since now it picks them up avidly right after I spread them out. But it's still pretty nervous and shy until I go back inside. Doesn't look like I'll get it to eat from my hand, though I've done it with other birds other places. It's almost spring, so the noble blue creature will probably be gone soon. I wonder which of its ancestors passed down the desire for this particular jay to hang around a bunch of old train cars for the winter?"

29.

Battle of the Web

Maybe you live in town or in a city and can relate better to
something smaller in the way of wildlife. How about the spider I
sort of had as a pet, one summer? Unfortunately, it was an unin-
vited pet, a black spider with a body as big as my thumbnail and
a muscular set of mountain legs to go with it. I generally don't
kill things I won't eat, unless they pose a threat to me or my family. That spider had an aggressive appearance, but I gave it the
benefit of the doubt and left it alone, so that we spent the following season living more or less in harmony with each other.

The spider actually lived outside, maintaining a big trampo-
line-looking web that almost completely spanned one of my caboose windows. It would crawl up and hide under the roof, waiting for a catch, coming out regularly to inspect and repair the set
up. The moment some unwary fly or bug bounced into the web
and got stuck, alarm bells went off in spidersville and the big
brute charged out to pummel the always-smaller victim senseless
(grabbing, biting, stabbing, whatever). It quickly wrapped up the
corpse with more strong webbing, stuck it over to one side, out of
the way, then repaired the main web so it would be ready to continue its work. Only after that would he carry his new victim up
under the roof to enjoy a repast.

Since my desk was right by the window where all this insec-
tual violence was taking place, I had little choice but to serve as
witness to quite a number of spider feasts, feeling somewhat like
a spectator at a Roman Circus. One day came the match-up of
the summer; one of those big, black, ugly looking wasps crashed
into this big, black, ugly looking spider's web, after which the two
tangled each other up for a while. The wasp was stuck to the web
by its wings, but still had its head and tail free, so the spider really had its own arms (or legs, I guess) full trying to get this latest
victim wrapped up. I went to the window, right up next to them,

to see the finer details of this battle, neither of them paying any attention to me at all. The wasp's antennas were swivelling furiously, while its sharp-pointed tail jabbed back and forth in an attempt to connect with the more deft spider.

Trying to get the big wasp wrapped up faster, the spider started tearing chunks of his webbing down, pulling the individual strands apart and rejoining them into the wasp's cocoon. But with one too many torn strings, the web got so weak it could no longer support the struggling pair, so the wasp suddenly broke free, tumbling downwards, all wrapped-up, for a foot or so before getting its wings freed enough to let it soar upwards and away.

At that point I wondered if spiders swear, and if so what this one might be saying, while it quickly went back to work patching up the big mangled web. About an hour later it was in operation, with the spider having probably worked up a pretty good appetite....

30.

A Human's Best Friend

There's not one of my country friends who lives without a dog. No wonder the dog food business is a multi-billion dollar industry; they've gotten enough from our family alone over the years to pay for somebody's limo. Dogs are most important, serving as our eyes and ears when we're indoors, barking variously according to the disturbances at hand. We don't like to keep dogs tied up, except as short term punishment when one or the other has run off too far or too long; they usually learn their lesson after a couple times of that. I strongly dislike dogs that bark endlessly, so we make a habit of going out to see what the cause is; if I feel it doesn't warrant all their racket I make sure to let them know. For this I reserve a tone of voice that's only used when I get mad. After a while I can stay indoors and that tone will usually make them stop. If not, I know it's worth getting up to investigate.

Tippy was perhaps our most beloved dog of all. Once we went for a morning walk in the middle of spring when she was about five and in her prime. As always, she stayed behind me obediently, wagging her tail with enthusiasm everytime I turned to look back, or even when I just I quietly spoke her name. If something got her too excited and she started to run, I only had to slap the side of my leg softly once or twice and she'd be right back behind me, or else beside me if the trail and terrain allowed it.

On this windy morning we walked north beyond the end of our field and on into the surrounding forest, following an overgrown road used by loggers years ago. We turned on a barely discernable branch road that dropped down to the next level of land, where by this time of year the rising river fed a small channel from which Tippy took a long drink. While thus engrossed, she didn't notice that a lone bush wolf was coming along a game trail on the other side of that water, not 75 feet away. He, in turn, was so busy watching his own trail that he didn't notice either one of us. He carried his right front paw up in the air, off the ground, apparently from some injury.

When that bush wolf got directly across from us it suddenly heard Tippy's loud slurping, just a dozen feet away, though a tall, thick bed of green reeds kept the two animals from seeing each other. But the bush wolf instantly recognized me as one of the dreaded humans, so it took off at top speed, even with only three good legs. I wished it well and said nothing to Tippy, who raised her head at about the same time and gave me a look of real satisfaction, water still dripping from her panting muzzle.

From there we went uphill to a nearby ridge, where we spooked a couple of blacktail deer who'd been grazing down in the lower reaches of their rocky cliffside domain. We didn't actually see them at first, we just heard their sounds, which were mixed in with other noises caused by the wind, so that it was hard to tell just where they were. However, being in the mood for adventure I took off in their direction, heading through a thin stand of little pines, where I ran smack-dab into a rusting remnant of that damned barbed wire fence put up by the guide who kept his horses here before we bought this land. The impact knocked me backwards and flat on the ground, nearly spraining my left wrist, putting a long scratch on the right one, and leaving me with a pretty sore neck as well. I was so stunned that for a few minutes I forgot all about chasing the deer; all I could do was mutter to myself about the fence, though I won't repeat any of what I said.

After going back home and licking my wounds for a while, so to speak, I took the canoe across our nearest river channel to explore one of the islands, surprised right away by the amount of elk and moose tracks so close within sight of our house and cabooses. Equally surprising was how quickly I found myself in an area I'd never visited before, even though this was now our tenth year here and I was less than five minutes from the bed where I sleep most every night. There's something very special about getting to know your own backyard, yet so many of us don't think much about it, even while we travel constantly to all manner of far away places.

This reminds me of another common question from visitors when they come around here. Looking at the fabulous Rocky Mountains, they sometimes wonder, "How many of those peaks have you climbed?" They seem disappointed when I answer, "none." My reason? Why go off exploring distant mountain tops when I haven't begun to know all the trails and places of interest within shouting distance of my own home? That's just a personal opinion, mind you, not necessarily a comment on those who prefer to fly across the world in order to hire a pack of natives to carry supplies to help them explore the backyards of other peoples. However, I will admit that I'm not usually impressed when I hear someone has reached another previously unconquered summit, nor do I get upset when they fall off and get killed during their efforts. I do grumble when these so-called "conquests" are of places whose people consider them sacred, especially when the "conquerors" despoil some of that sacredness in the process, then offer what's left of it to the rest of the world as trophies, or as challenges for others to outdo.

Coming back from those islands in my canoe, I spooked up a couple of mallard ducks and their ducklings, a scene that would have made a nice photo, though I rarely carry a camera on these outings, preferring to enjoy nature with my own senses, rather than through a mechanical device. The elder ducks flew up from the water, while the little ones swam in a silent beeline toward the reeds, where they quickly disappeared, after which their folks passed by again overhead, as ducks often do, either to see what was happening with their offspring or else just as some inherited function of retracing their escape route (a sad mistake when the intruder comes not just to watch, but armed with a shotgun).

After half an hour of paddling towards the main river channel and seeing nothing, I turned back and headed home, encountering the two older ducks again as they swam slowly along the reeds where they'd last seen their kids, quietly calling out to them, "Wuk, wuk, wuk." I steered far enough around so as not to alarm them this time, then watched from the bank as the little duck family was reunited and went on with their diving for food and general frolicking.

Tippy had waited at the landing for me all this time, dozing silently while nature cavorted all around. Together we walked back towards the house when suddenly a big whitetail deer jumped out of the brush and ran uphill just ahead of us. It stopped near the top to look back, while at the same instant my dog found an old bone at her feet, which interested her more than the deer, so she picked it up and checked to see if it was hers (I'm sure it was), and to taste if there was anything left to get from it. During those moments everything remained silent, neither of us really moved, so the deer bent its head down as if it were grazing, though I knew that at least one eye and both ears were still fully tuned towards us. At that point Tippy started crunching on that bone with her teeth, at which the deer instantly straightened up and fixed its full attention on us again. Then a second deer came out of the bush and joined the first one in looking our way, though Tippy saw none of that, being now fully involved in the crunching of that bone. Had the two deer caught our scent they would have run away instantly, but a gentle breeze was blowing in the wrong direction, so they tried again to continue with their grazing, though they'd obviously lost their taste for food and were more concerned with taking glances at us. Sometimes their big ears twitched in harmony with Tippy's noisy bone crunching, making me wonder if that bone might once have been a relative of theirs.

Tippy was actually a pretty alert dog most of the time, so I was surprised at her sudden overwhelming interest in this old bone. Finally I hissed quietly, which was my signal to let her know something was around. On my second effort she dropped the bone and went on alert, but she still didn't notice the two brown and white faces staring directly at us, less than 100 feet away, somewhat camouflaged by the green and brown of the forest. But the dog's sudden interest made the deer even more nervous, so they raised their white tails stiffly and moved them slowly from side to side - signalling that they were about to bolt. Combined with another hiss from me, this finally got Tippy to figure out what was going on. She stared very hard at the two deer, though still none of us moved. For some reason the deer then lowered their white tails, at which point Tippy sat down on her haunches, maybe figuring to watch the two deer some more, but that move was apparently one too many. Cautiously, the closest of the pair lifted first one foot, then the other, slowly making its way *towards* us, instead of running away! Now this time it was getting too much for Tippy, who would have preferred to run and chase after them. Knowing my strong feelings on that subject, she simply turned her attention back to the old bone and began chewing on it again as if nothing was happening, being even more noisy about it than before. Meanwhile, all that standing around in the late afternoon breeze had started to make me feel chilly, so I decided to head back to work inside my caboose, nervous deer or not. As soon as I took a step towards them both deer ran, bounding up the hill and over several big bushes with graceful leaps until they were out of sight. When Tippy and I got up to the meadow ourselves, they were already back to grazing, not more than a hundred feet away. From there, they watched us walk to my caboose, heard my footsteps on the platform and the squeaking of the door, yet when I looked out from the cupola about an hour later, just before it got completely dark, they were still grazing in the same place, while Tippy was laying down between the ties underneath my caboose, determined as ever to chew up that new found old bone.

One winter day some years ago I gave our dogs a big red apple that was pretty wrinkled and far gone for human consumption. I figured it would take some of the monotony out of the cold day if they chewed on this, expecting to bring out a couple more if the first one was well received. At that time we still had our all time favorite Tippy, a border collie mama with black hair and a stout body, along with a partly golden face and underside, same as her five year old pups Boss and Baby. Tippy took that apple willingly, as she did most anything that came from *my* hands, but she dropped it the moment I turned and left, then sniffed it a couple more times before walking away. Each of the other two dogs then went over and checked it out, sniffed it, took a taste of it, but also left it. I figured our dogs were just not as smart about this as old Mr. Wloka's German Shepherd, who eats apples eagerly, big and ripe, right in their orchard.

For the next couple of days Tippy adopted that red apple as sort of a pet, carrying it along whenever she followed me back and forth between my studio at the caboose and the house. Suddenly on one of those trips she dropped the apple on the trail and walked away from it, as if she'd had enough. I figured it was a good time to get rid of this piece of disgrace, giving it a good kick way out into the field, where I hoped that maybe some birds would eat what was left. I don't think it even quit rolling before old Tippy had run and pounced on it, grabbing it excitedly between her teeth, which made me laugh out loud. I had gone up to the house on that occasion to stoke the fire and bring in fresh water while the family was in town. As I filled the two buckets at the hand pump all three dogs were jumping around, being playful, as were the three cats that we had at the time. Tippy still had the apple at this point, and somehow that now seemed to excite all the others. When I headed back to my caboose she came right behind, and when I stopped for a short pause on the way, she dropped the apple again and stood beside me patiently, as if letting her mouth rest from it.

The other two dogs came over to her, one at a time, wagging their tails playfully, though it was obvious that their main interest suddenly was again in checking out that red thing in their mama's mouth. She wagged her tail back at them, but growled each time one showed its true intentions regarding the apple, which caused them to back off at once. After that we continued towards my caboose, the three dogs behind me, and the cats further back, all of us strung out in single file.

Suddenly Tippy stopped, let the apple fall once again, then clamped down on it hard with one paw, after which she tore it apart and ate it completely. This was too much for the pups, who jumped around her excitedly. Baby, always the sneakier of the two, managed to get one piece that fell from Tippy's mouth while she was chewing. Apples were suddenly in style, as Baby chewed up that piece with gusto, while more hesitant brother Boss managed only to find a really tiny apple scrap, which he slurped out of the snow with his tongue enthusiastically, thus able to join the other two in a great round of tail wagging to show satisfaction.

I reached down to pet Tippy and congratulate her for a meal well done but this got the other two riled up and also yearning for attention, so I rubbed my hands together quickly and made certain noises with my tongue that always got them hyped up even more. Finally I told Tippy "sic 'em! sic 'em!" Instead of barking and looking into the distance, as she usually did in response, this time she turned on the nearest living thing, which happened to be her shy son Boss, who freaked out and ran off down the trail, no doubt wondering what that red thing had done to his mom and I. Baby immediately turned and joined her brother, thus making the cats think both dogs were coming after them. In response they clambered up the nearest trees while the pups continued running and barking all the way back to the house. Old Tippy then sauntered over to me with her usual happy look - we called it a smile - wagging her tail, then laying down contentedly between the railroad ties under my caboose, which was often her favorite fair weather place.

During that same winter I enjoyed another little incident with the dogs that I considered worthy of recording. One day I watched from the window by my desk aboard the caboose as Tippy came down the trail from the house proudly bearing a new bone with bits of meat still clinging to it. She stopped at my woodpile, just past the caboose steps, looking for a place where she could bury the bone, a popular practice of hers. Nothing seemed right, so she headed further down the trail, towards the boxcars and other cabooses, stopping every few steps to look both right and left, but still nothing seemed to suit her.

She was a couple of car lengths away already when her son Boss showed up on the trail, obviously eager to see what his dear mama was gonna do with that scrumptious looking bone. He either didn't get one of his own, or his smaller but sneakier sister Baby snatched it away, in which case he would have been too shy to go and take it back from her. At any rate, he happened to be in trouble with me, for having run off into the woods with his sister, possibly chasing elk, which I forbid them quite sternly from doing. When they were young I tied them up whenever they did it. This was the first occasion in a long time, so I just growled at them each time I saw them away from the house, which had the desired effect. On this day, it made Boss pull in his tail and trot back home before he could even learn where his mom had ended up burying that bone. She looked under the kids' caboose while Boss was still on her trail, but after he ran off she came back out with the bone still in her mouth. It was enjoyable watching this whole silent episode, since it seemed very apparent that Tippy was really "thinking" each spot out carefully, doing it in her own way. I don't normally see our dogs around here "thinking;" generally they seem to operate on the impulse principle instead. In Tippy's case, it almost seems as though she realized I was watching and she didn't want me to know either, since during the blink of an eye she disappeared for a few minutes, then came trotting back towards my caboose with the treasure somewhere stashed.

"Home alone and being entertained by an interesting trio outside my window," says a note in another journal about one of our earlier dogs, Arrow. "He's outside putting up with two magpies who have nothing better to do than to harass a poor lonesome dog (we just had the one for a time). They take turns buzzing over him quite close, then landing nearby and pretending to eat something, until Arrow runs over to see what it is. Just before he reaches them they fly up, then sit and watch him from one of the big pine trees out front, as he sniffs around eagerly, expecting to find whatever it was they were eating. Could it be that those magpies have a sense of humor; that maybe they laugh quietly inside? They definitely seemed to enjoy making the poor dog look foolish."

One winter I was reading nightly bedtime stories for the kids from Jack London's *Call of the Wild,* which really fired up Okan and Iniskim's enthusiasm for dogsleds and snow. It so happened that Tippy had her only litter of pups at this time, so I agreed to let the boys each keep and raise one.

"Iniskim and I decided to name our two pups Baby and Boss, and to teach them to pull a sled," Okan remembers. "We were about nine and ten, and didn't really know how to go about this. But there were some drawings in the book and based on them we got our mom to sew us a set of harnesses using canvas, with metal rings.

"We first trained the dogs to be led on leashes, then later we put the harness on them. It was hooked to a sled that we made ourselves from an old pair of skis on top of which we put a box frame. One of us would ride on the sled by standing on the back of the runners, holding on to a wooden handlebar, while the other ran ahead and led the dogs. Unfortunately, we never got them really trained to pull by verbal commands, so about the only time they would open up and go fast without one of us leading in front was when we were heading home after a long ride."

In hindsight, Okan says he should have read a sled-dog training book before getting started. He now knows much different training techniques, with more benefit both for the dogs and himself. Also, he would have known to get a proper sled and harness right at the start, though they did make some better ones later on. Overall, the experience gave them a unique learning experience, but Okan still feels unfulfilled, yearning someday to get a proper team of dogs and try dog sledding again.

A seldom mentioned but common problem for country folks is the training of young dogs to learn the rules of a place. Few country homes have the luxury of a tall surrounding fence to keep dogs in, so country pups have to learn pretty quick that they better stick around home. We haven't had one yet that didn't test us on this a few times, making it a problem that's still looking for a better solution. Whenever I've caught one of ours in the act of chasing, I've scolded them severly and tied them up, which seems to make them more willing to settle down. I think what really causes problems for wildlife are dogs whose owners don't look after them at all, plus dogs who are outright strays, often chasing wildlife out of genuine need and hunger.

One time when Boss and Baby were about five or six they stayed away all morning. Now and then I could hear them barking about half a mile away, which told me they were up to no good. By then I'd learned that there was no use to chase after them because they were way quicker, and once they saw me they'd get scared and would refuse to stop. So, I told Star to watch for their return and let me know, since I was writing down at my caboose.

Sure enough, after a while she called me, having ridden her bike down with the two now-returned dogs following her. Their tongues were hanging way out the sides of their mouths as I climbed down the caboose steps with a short stick, at first pretending I didn't notice them. They'd learned that if I looked at them with anger they'd best make a run for it, but in this case they stood still until I was close enough to smack them both on their rumps, scolding them loudly at the same time. Knowing that Baby was the main instigator of these unwelcome departures, I grabbed her by the collar and gave her a couple of extra whacks, grumbling in a stern voice, while she did her best to look pitiful. That was too much for Cleo, our calico cat, who must have had her own complaints about Baby, though I couldn't say what they were. When she saw what was happening and heard the dog yelping with fright, she couldn't resist racing out from under the caboose and diving on poor hapless Baby herself, claws out, hissing and spitting.

My adrenalin was already flowing pretty strong, so I gave the ferocious cat a whack with the same stick, then threw a couple more on the dog for good measure, after which I let her go. She took off on the homeward trail, running to her old mama, not far behind Boss, who was trying to catch up with Star on her bike. Star later said she was feeling cheap about this time for luring the dogs down only to get them a beating, then felt even worse when she saw her cat getting a whack as well. The cat, meanwhile, realizing she was unhurt from the stick, was now even more peeved at the dog, so she tore after the whole crew, letting out a mad cat scream in the process, then running so fast cross country that she soon caught up to those on the trail ahead, in the process leaping right up on Baby's back while hissing so loudly that I could hear it clearly, way down the field. The dog managed to knock the cat off and continue, but the cat still didn't have enough. Passing Star on her bike, she caught the dog once more with a wild mid-air jump, whereupon Baby decided she'd been pushed around enough. She floored the cat, then grabbed it between her teeth and gave it a pretty vicious shaking. Beverly came out to baby her Star, while Baby the dog had to crawl down under the house to find her own mama and try to get some comfort, not being seen by us again until late the next day. That would have made one heck of a video sequence!

As if that weren't enough animal capers, I watched an even better performance a while later through my binoculars, sitting in the upstairs comfort of my caboose's cupola. It was early in the spring, so there were about a dozen elk grazing on fresh green grass out on our field, partway between the tracks and the old family house. There were also quite a few birds on the ground, mainly feeding on the bugs being scared up by the grazing elk.

A yearling bull with short horns was about ten feet from a particular robin, not very far from me, when I noticed that his head was actually following along with the hopping bird as if he were mesmerized by it. When the bird turned to the left, so did the elk, and when it turned quickly to the right, he did that too. I laughed, thinking it was a momentary coincidence, but then I realized that elk was really getting into it. Obviously the bird realized it too, or else it surely would have flown away. Presumably it knew that elk are harmless, giving me a private performance of a unique robin and elk ballet.

The robin began to hop further by using its wings, twisting and turning all the while, as that elk went ahead and slowly made a fool of himself, going overboard in front of his whole herd, trying to duplicate the bird's movements, hopping around and prancing in ways I've never seen any other elk do. Had he been a mature bull we would have all been impressed - the cows, the birds and I - but I'm sure each one of us has seen other young elk running around and acting silly, so we were only left to wonder how this guy came to be the Harpo Marx of them all.

Several times during this fandango the bird and elk got within a few inches of each other, but in the end the bird won. It suddenly flew right up into the elk's face, getting him so freaked out that he jumped into the air with all four legs, then came back down crooked, so that he lost his footing and crashed. At that point the robin flew up into the lower branches of the nearest pine tree, followed by most of the other birds. The bull got back up, then went over and stood underneath that tree, looking up at his robin friend quizzically, as if to say, "Now why'd you go and spoil the fun we were having by scaring me like that?" The nearest other elk also looked up at the bird in the tree, but all the rest had long since gone back to their grazing. I made a note that this episode took about six minutes and would have made an even better piece of video than the previous tale.

One trouble with having well loved family dogs is that you're sure to have heartaches with them. It's a pitiful thing to watch life slowly drain from a faithful old four legged companion, as if it were a child too soon grown old.

The biggest heartache I recall was with Tippy, who suffered a real winter calamity when she was about twelve years old. The first sign of it came when she didn't greet me, after I'd been gone a couple days for a funeral. It was after dark when I got home and the thermometer was at -25F, so I wasn't surprised that neither Tippy nor her two kids came out; on nights like that they preferred to curl up together deep under the house and not move unless necessary. I went inside and had a short visit with the boys, then went down to my caboose, lit a fire, and settled in for the night, planning to get an early and undisturbed start the next day on my writing work.

Okan showed up after daybreak with my breakfast of porridge, bundled up tightly for the wickedly icy cold. "Is Tippy down here with you?" he asked. I suddenly recalled the moment's concern I'd felt for her the previous night. It was way too cold for her to be under my caboose, where there was only some straw between the ties, while under the house there was a sheltered dog nest. I decided to walk back up with him so we could have a look. Unfortunately, drifted snow was piled around and frozen so solid that we couldn't actually see back to where the dogs liked to lay. But when we called Tippy, only Boss and Baby showed up, eagerly wagging their tails. Things looked very serious, but what could we do? There were no fresh tracks leading away from the house, and a recent snowfall made other signs too unclear. I went back to my caboose with a heavy heart.

Tippy had one mighty big problem alright: it appears she'd gotten too wide in the hips to use her old route under the front porch in order to reach the sheltered straw nest, especially with that added layer of snow that had blown under the porch during the last storm. She made it partway, before getting stuck sideways under a support beam. The boys finally discovered her, so we quickly grabbed crowbars and hammers to tear the porch apart, no easy task since the boards were tightly expanded from the cold and the whole thing was frozen solid. Once we had enough of it broken to see her clearly, it gave us a deep shock. She was still alive, but laying in a puddle of snow and mud that had melted from her body heat, while her thick black hair and most of her body extremities were frozen down solidly. She could barely lift her head, and a bit of her front quarters.

Okan and I took turns cutting her hair with his hunting knife, pulling upwards on her body as gently as possible to pry her loose. Most of her beautiful tail was frozen down, but she wagged what she could of it, though barely. It took the three of us some time in that bitter cold just to get that poor dog free, after which we brought her into the house on a blanket and laid her inside an open wooden crate that we had on hand. Dogs aren't normally allowed in our house, for religious reasons, but in this case we made an exception. Unfortunaly she was beyond caring about this special treat. We made sure to keep her in the coolest corner, far from the heater, since she was obviously suffering from a dog's version of hypothermia, if not outright bodily freezing. It was about noon by the time we got her settled and stabilized, figuring to let nature decide the course of things. Even if we'd wanted to bring her to a vet, it would have been more risk and trouble in that weather than I was willing to take, and I don't think she would have survived it. Instead I laid and hugged her gently, until she closed her eyes and more or less passed out from all her struggles. I told the boys that the next 24 hours would be crucial; if she could pull through for that long I figured she'd make it.

It was impossible for me to write that afternoon, though I sat for quite a while and tried to force myself. Finally one of the boys came down to say that Tippy was awake, but unable to get up or stand. I again rushed back to the house, dreading whatever was to come next, feeling awful as I stood and stared at her lying so helplessly at my feet. Her tail wagged feebly when I knelt down beside her, so I picked up her face and held it gently between my hands, crying with pity for this dear friend. After a bit she started whining with me, just lightly, then she managed to lift one of her paws enough to rest it on the wrist of my hand, which made me cry even more.

What was especially painful about Tippy's plight is that we had all been warm and comfortable in our beds, while our faithful old family dog was trapped outside in the coldest night, frozen to the ground, every minute no doubt in terror and agony. But, wonder of wonders, the old girl slowly pulled herself back....

The next morning I got up early and headed to the house for breakfast. On the way, I watched as the boys came out and went to the woodshed, followed soon after by Boss, or so I thought. When I got near I was amazed to realize it was Tippy, determined to follow them although obviously having a hard time of it. At least she was up and about. This time my tears were for joy. She tried to squat in the deep snow but only managed to collapse. In addition to her general weakness, she was unable to use her right front paw, which was held off the ground and just hung there. She had tripped a couple of times on her way out because of it. It was vital for her to hold up long enough to practice her bodily functions, but she couldn't do it on this try. She barely made it back to the house, especially the last part which involves going up on a porch and then up again through the doorway. She sort of fell into the house, a sad thing for a fine old dog. After we got her back to bed she was even unable to lift her head for the next half hour or so.

We kept after her, especially the boys, making her go outside every few hours to keep her from getting too stiff or giving up. It constantly looked like a toss-up between recovery and death. In fact, at one point while I was alone with her she suddenly forced herself to get up, standing on both front feet with legs held really stiff, her body kind of crooked. Then her eyes began to glaze over and her body started trembling, so I thought her time had come. Wanting to let her die in comfort, I hugged her and held her to my chest, at which point she collapsed fully into my arms. Again I thought she was gone, but to my amazement she started looking more normal instead, and from that point on her recovery was continuous.

But there were other complications. About a week later we discovered that deep within the remaining thick winter hair, the old dog had an open sore big enough to stick my finger into; I could only bear to glance at it briefly. We decided a vet was now needed, so mama and the kids took the mama dog into town. I feared she had gangrene from being frozen for so long and it meant some possible amputation. She'd been doing so good until a day or so before we noticed the wound, when she suddenly got weak and gloomy again, limping and having a hard time just to rise. The vet checked her over and gave her some medicine, which did the trick with her hip in just a few days. He figured she had a stroke that time when I held her, after all the trauma of the freezing. Tough old girl, she nevertheless held on for two more years after that, pretty much an old lady version of what she'd always been, with no real specific disability from her icy trauma.

A summer treat for me through the years when Tippy was our main family dog was to go berry picking with her, saskatoons mainly, she eating from the low branches and me picking from the higher. Sometimes we'd both stop and look at each other chewing mouthfuls of purple berries, communicating without words how delicious they were. She always plucked them very daintily from the branches, catching hardly a green leaf between her teeth.

Tippy used to take food from my hand in the same gentle manner, a custom I taught her after she grew beyond the initial puppy habit of grabbing food and gulping it down. I made note of how one time I'd given Tippy half a bakery bun on which I'd smeared some raspberry jam. When I first stepped outdoors with it and held the bun up high, she assumed it was mine, so she totally ignored it while knowing full well that it was there. When I said her name she instantly focused on me, but still made no sign that she was in any way expecting to get the treat. Slowly I lowered it down towards her head, while she sat proudly and wagged her tail. When it got near, I began to tell her in a quiet voice how good that bun was going to taste, which made her tail wag even more furiously, while the tip of her tongue kept darting out and giving a quick lick over her chops. When the bun got within an inch of her nose she sniffed towards it gingerly and tried to wag her tail even harder, if that was possible, but she still never opened her mouth nor made any other attempt to take it until I held it right at her lips and told her the right Blackfoot word. Had I said to her in English, "here," she still wouldn't have touched it. When she finally lipped it from my fingers, she did it with such slow and deliberate motion that she seemed to be hypnotized, or else was trying to hypnotize me. When she was sure it was hers, she walked away several steps to a place where the grass looked green and soft. There she dropped it gently, sniffed it carefully again, turned it over with one paw so that the jam side was up, then began licking it *very* methodically. After a bit of this licking she paused to look up at me, as if to make sure she was to have the rest of it, too. Feeling reassured, she layed down, put her front paws on both sides of the bun, then began taking small nibbles from its corners, apparently savoring each sweetened, pre-licked bite. In those days, if her two grown kids had come around, there would have been a mad dash for mama's treat, but they were dozing somewhere else without any disturbance.

My notes on this bun-eating incident concluded by saying it was "truly an artistic performance of a dog eating style," and that it made my gift of the bun seem especially appreciated. I ended that day feeling extra good about life, and giving thanks for getting to know Tippy.

Beverly had her own special fondness for Tippy, since the dog grew up with Star and served as a reliable babysitter for our kids in the early years when they liked to go out into the wilds by themselves for exploring. "I always felt safe when Tippy was with the kids, and lots of country mothers will know how much that means," she says in recognition.

As Tippy got older she had a harder time each winter with the cold and snow. Beverly brought Tippy inside whenever it got too cold. The dog seemed to appreciate this tremendously, though she never fully adapted to indoor life and would get up anytime during the night to let us know she wanted out. If everyone was sleeping too soundly, she'd go to the back door and use her teeth to try chewing her way out, resulting in more than a few carpentry repairs. However, on the day when her end finally came, she could no longer get up, and that night she crawled as close to Beverly's bed as she could get, where she quietly breathed her last.

A devoted trio, with Tippy on the right,
Baby at left and humble Boss in the background

31.

A Father and Son Hike Across the Rockies

At a dance on the Blood Indian Reserve I was invited to a pow-wow among the neighboring Stoney people by my adopted sister, Myna Lefthand and her husband Carl. Their small Eden Valley Reserve happens to be almost directly east of our homestead, with only the Rocky Mountains in between. Without hesitation I told them, "Sure, we'll even walk there!" Myna laughed and said she'd watch for my arrival, but later admitted that she thought I was kidding.

Actually, I'd been looking for an excuse to hike across the Rockies since the previous season, when I happened to get hold of an old anthropologist's field map that included our region and showed many Indian campsites and trails, pencilled in during several visits with tribal elders of the Kootenays in the 1930's. Our own homestead used to be an old Indian campground, and Myna's Eden Valley Reserve was the same for her Stoney people. The trails connecting us and them seemed well marked on the map, so I figured this was an ideal opportunity to see traditional country that remains relatively unchanged from far back times.

Among my boys, eight-year old Okan got especially enthused when I asked who would join me, his younger brother Iniskim gamely saying he'd come along too. So we fixed up three packs with sleeping bags, spare clothes and a bit of grub, the main part of which was dried meat from an elk I'd shot the previous year, plus some granola and dried fruits. I didn't want to bring much since I figured to move right along on this trip and spend little time camping and cooking. I packed our tent in addition to my own gear, plus a tarp to put over it in case of rain.

Earlier I mentioned how romantic ideals about the outdoors often have to give way to reality. In this case, I wanted to walk directly from our tipi to another tipi set up by my sister on the far side of the mountains. My ideal was to make this a primitive adventure; just our feet and nature, leaving the modern world behind. Unfortunately, the only logical route from our valley bottom up into the ranges of the Rockies is along a stretch of steep logging road, where the noise, dust and danger from passing truck traffic would not make a pleasant beginning for the hike, so we hesitantly agreed to drive beyond that area with our four-wheel drive crew cab truck.

At the end of the road our whole family camped together on the shore of a pretty little mountain lake. According to the map, upstream from there an old Kootenay trail would bring us to the headwaters of a creek and from there through a pass and over the Rockies. We got an early start the next morning, though there was no sign of any trail near the creek so we had to make our own way through dense brush and over fallen timber. Thank heavens the whole family decided to come along with us for the first part, since it soon became apparent that Iniskim was still too small to make it through rugged terrain, especially with a pack, and with the *real* climbing yet ahead. There were a few tears as he turned back with Mama and older brother Wolf, leaving just me and Okan, along with our anthropologist's map.

Before long the thick brush tore one of the two shoulder straps off my new pack, at which point I sat down somewhat frustrated and wondered if this big idea of following an old map was going to work. I sometimes face similar doubts at the start of a new book, when many a bright idea gets a dose of reality and looks much dimmer. But perserverance generally pays off in both kinds of cases, so I got out my sewing kit, stitched the strap back on, then continued our rough climb with new determination.

Rather than follow the creek bed to its head, I eventually decided to get us up out of the dark timber, with its endless jumble of downed trees, though that meant climbing very steeply for the next couple of hours. We were going up one of two mountains that showed on the map as flanking both the creek and trail, though the pencil marks were indecisive enough that the correct route could be anywhere in the area. We were quite deep into the

Rocky Mountain ranges and theoretically surrounded by nothing but wilderness, yet the air was continually pierced by the distant wailing of chainsaws doing their vicious business. The higher we got, the more the forest thinned out; all we saw were small trees, though huge old stumps in the ground showed how much different the forest might have looked before the era of logging. It never ceases to amaze me that so many humans are willing to make radical changes to their environment without really considering the long term consequences, even in these supposedly environmentally-enlightened 1990's. I hope reliable polls soon show that people like this have become a minority and that those of us who favor the protection of nature are growing stronger. Pardon my digression, but to me this has got to be the world's number one concern.

We were climbing an oddly shaped mountain, eventually coming out at its top, where it ended with a sheer ridge. In the dark we might have kept on going, stepping over an edge that dropped straight down into a *very* deep canyon, with at least a couple thousand feet to the bottom. Such heights are not my favorite places (I hope my Swiss forefathers aren't listening), so I crawled up to the edge of this one on my belly, got rather sweaty and short of breath, then layed still for as long as I dared in order to look straight down and take in that very awesome view. It was obvious that, *had* we stayed along the creek bed, we'd have found ourselves way down there in a walled-in, dead-end basin, the creek bed being the only way in and out.

We moved back from the edge and sat by some bushes to consider our options. We could go back the way we'd come and try to locate another route, else we could go on down the other side of this mountain and hope from there to find a better route leading us further. Unfortunately, there were no definite trails anywhere, though lots of bear signs, including freshly torn stumps, rolled over logs, and trampled berry bushes, along with boulders recently moved by something a great deal stronger than us two put together. We had to travel on faith through the thick brush, deep in grizzly country. To compound our situation it started raining, so we tried going faster, with Okan doing a good job of keeping up, though he later admitted that the whole time he was getting gloomier. I had no chance to do the same, since I was in charge and had to worry about where we'd end up and what we needed to avoid while getting there. Now and then we stopped and silently stared at huge excavations of dirt and rock, as though a couple of busy miners had been determined to find gold. We didn't want to catch the maker of these in the process, since it would be a grizzly, and it probably wouldn't notice us until perhaps too late.

Once I thought I heard a sob behind me, but when I turned to look everything seemed to be alright. Okan later admitted he'd been feeling so bad about the hard, wet hike, going along without even a trail, plus the absence of his little brother, that he felt his face "kind of twist up" which is when that sob accidentally came out. However, he was determined to get control of it, a trait he has continued to practice. He told me this later, while we paused on the other side of that mountain (which we learned is over 8,000 feet high). We had another talk about what to do, thinking that maybe instead of crossing the Rockies to the east, we might just head south and enter the Bull River valley near its headwaters, a wild region we'd also heard about but never got a chance to visit. There are old Indian camping and hunting sites in that area too, the idea of which cheered us up, but then we remembered that the rest of our family would be driving over to meet us at the pow-wow camp; they'd get worried if we didn't show up. Suddenly we heard nearby motor sounds, loud and ugly to our ears. In a few more steps we came out onto a wide trail that showed signs of having been used recently by all-terrain vehicles. Three young fellows on dirt bikes came roaring up, the first two going right by us, but the last one skidding to a halt, in the process of which he fell over. Walking his bike back to us with a limp, he asked in a loud, alcohol-tinged voice if there was any other way "back to Elkford" than this particular trail, though I told him I didn't know. After he roared off I told Okan that we now had the right route, since our first night's destination was an old Indian campground called Round Prairie, right next to Elkford. All we had to do now was go to where they'd come from, knowing that if their bikes made it, our feet certainly would too. That anthropologist has no idea how much trouble he caused just by putting his pencil line one creek too far over! When the rain stopped, we paused at one of the numerous clear streams, drank plenty of water and ate a few bites of food. Okan was already so worn out that he even slept for a few minutes, after which we took off with renewed vigor. The trail had become a forest road, though it was no longer open to vehicle traffic. There were some nearly impassable rocky sections, which took some time for us to cross. No wonder that fellow had asked us about another way back; dragging dirt bikes across would have been something worth seeing, especially if they were already drinking by then.

We stopped at another creek for a drink of water when a dog suddenly ran up, followed a few seconds later by a sprightly, bearded fellow wearing only running shoes and jogging shorts, plus a sweater tied around his waist. I was perplexed, wondering if we had gone from the Canadian Rockies to New York's Central Park.

This gent's name was Gunnar Kahn, and he'd gotten lost too; well, not lost, but he'd gone that morning looking for the same lake by which our family was camped, then taken the wrong road (which happened to be the one Okan and I *should* have followed). He was now on his way back home to Elkford and knew of the old Indian campground we were seeking, offering to walk there with us. He insisted on carrying my pack, after he heard about our great mistake. He said the added weight would give him more exercise, an attitude from which many of us would benefit. In turn, I took Okan's lighter pack, which sure cheered him up and made him more lively for the rest of the day.

As the trail got higher up into a pass, we stopped to eat some of the berries growing everywhere. There were little strawberries. tasting really sweet, though we had to gather many of them just to make a decent mouthful. We also sampled gooseberries and muleberries, though these were smaller and not yet fully ripe. Tiny mountain blueberries grew really close to the ground, making them hard to get without taking off our packs. My own favorite as always, were the raspberries. I've never tasted any more delicious than these way up in the high mountains. They were quite abundant, some being as big as my thumb nail. No wonder we saw signs of bears wherever we looked.

It was nearly dark when we finally reached Round Prairie, the ancient campsite being located on a grassy meadow in a bend of the Elk River. We quickly put up our tent and spread out our sleeping bags, then got undressed and jumped into the icy current to wash off the day's miseries after which we felt much better. We spent the next while sitting around a little campfire, going back over the trails in our minds, without the physical miseries.

We slept good, though it rained on and off, waking us up to a wet, gloomy and cloudy scene. About the time we got everything packed up, our friend Gunnar showed up with a four wheel drive Toyota and offered us a ride. He'd checked with a local old timer about our proposed route and came to tell us that the anthropologist had not been much of a mapmaker, since even the main pass we'd intended to use was no good. It has a clear trail going up *our* side to the top, but his old timer friend insisted there was no way back down on the other side. Between them they thought we might end up spending a lot of time reaching the summit only to end up coming back the same way.

The crossing to use instead was Fording Pass, north from our intended route, and - as it later turned out - actually the main route used back in old times by Kootenay and Stoney Indians who wanted to visit each other. To reach this pass we had to share the narrow valley with a good road that was used by heavy trucks coming down from nearby coal mines. Gunnar offered to drive us a few miles beyond that road so we could go on with our walk in peace and safety. Since rain was now coming down steadily, his offer was too good to refuse. There was nothing to see for the next 40 miles anyhow, except dark, wet forests, banks of low clouds obscuring any views we might have had of the tall mountain peaks that our friend assured us were all around.

Our road trip ended on the shore of the Elk River, where a bridge had been taken out. Beyond there we'd be back in pure wilderness, but first we had to cross the rain-swollen river. It's good to have memorable adventures with your own kids, but these don't need to include taking an eight-year old across a wide, icy river. I considered making two trips across, one with the packs and the other with Okan, but the brave boy assured me he'd be alright on his own. We held hands and carried sturdy walking sticks, but the water's force was so strong that several times it nearly got the best of us, especially since our legs grew more numb with each minute in the cold. Fortunately, we were both used to daily cold baths in the river channel back home, so we managed to reach the other side with no problem. It sure felt good to put warm socks back on our shocked feet.

There were more river crossings ahead, but as we climbed higher they became progressively narrower, until we could cross them by stepping on rocks and finally just by jumping across. Towards the summit our trail grew incredibly steep, so that we could look almost straight up to where it disappeared into misty clouds, reminding me of Himalayan views from magazines. The day was rainy enough to make this steep trail so slippery that for each step we took forward we slid nearly half of that back. It was slow, sometimes frustrating, then again breathtaking. What we didn't know was that the mists had hidden from view the fact that this trail went up nearly again that far, cresting a major mountain range in which lay our intended pass.

The clouds opened enough to give us sunshine and an awesome view near the top of this grade. A very rugged and treeless domain, so much different from our riverside meadows back home, though waters from here soon flow down to where we live. Fresh animal tracks were everywhere, and of all kinds, including elk, moose, mountain goat, bighorn sheep and of course black bears and grizzlies. This was not an area where they passed through once in a while, it was the place they lived most the time. Behind every tree and bush there could be one, this knowledge adding zest to our hike. Even when nothing showed itself we were left wondering what might have watched our passing in silence.

The pass itself was an even more spectacular place, letting us look back towards our cloud covered valley and up ahead to a vast blue sky that sheltered the spreading prairie beyond the craggy peaks. And peaks there were, many and in all directions, most not much higher up than we, everything here being above the treeline. A strong, cold wind was blowing, and fierce black clouds were swirling about. Rather than linger, we started down the eastern slope of the Rockies, thrilled that with each step the weather got nicer. Looking towards our destination, Okan said, "That sure is an inviting sight, so brightly lit after our days with rain and clouds."

There was only one thing that kept this wilderness experience from being complete - someone had already come and taken noticeable little bits of the mountain top with them. Here and there along the stony trail were inch-thick holes made by some kind of machine for the purpose of seeing what kind of minerals there are deep inside. What a rude intrusion into nature - at least they could have sealed those holes back up. Instead, looks like they'll remain forever as technological graffiti in a pristine range.

That night we made our camp along the Highwood River, which we reached after dark, having travelled through a long rugged stretch that had no inviting campsites. Fortunately we didn't know until later at the pow-wow camp that on this same day a very large grizzly had been live trapped in the next creekbed over from the one our trail followed down. All we saw were deer, including a very large antlered buck who acted completely unafraid of us.

We reached the tipi camp the next day, after sleeping in, then drying our bedding in the warm sun. We took another dip in the river, on whose shore we found a well-weathered twenty dollar bill, leaving us to wonder how it had gotten there. The tipi camp was then just forming, and the area was otherwise remote for most people.

The first person we met was Johnny Lefthand, an elderly uncle of sister Myna's husband, who was helping his wife set up a tipi. They greeted us with warmth and friendship, all the more so when they learned that we'd just walked over from our home in B.C. We sat on the ground next to Johnny, who was sharpening some wooden stakes.

The Lefthands' tipi had horses painted around the outside of it, fitting for a well-known old cowboy like Johnny. He talked about the trip of his lifetime, when he was one of four Canadian Indian cowboys chosen in 1939 to visit Australia and teach riding and rodeo skills. Johnny Lefthand was a successful rodeo cowboy back then, famous for his bronc riding, steer decorating and calf roping. In 1932 he was the All-Around Champion at the world famous Calgary Stampede.

The quiet and humble personality of Johnny Lefthand doesn't indicate that, for much of his life, he's also been a noted leader of his Stoney people, a man who successfully took on federal government bureaucracy to become perhaps the last chief of a Plains Indian tribe to lead a group of followers to settle on their own piece of ancestral land. This stands as an example of what a small group of people can accomplish in nature when they set their minds on a common goal and remain committed to it.

"My trip to Australia taught me a lot more about the world than most of my people knew in those days," Johnny told us, "and it let me see how other people live. When I came back home I realized that our tribe was not doing so well on the reserve at Morley (near Calgary, about an hour away). It was a beautiful piece of land, right close to Banff National Park, but there was no work for us or any way to improve our living. My own family came from south of that reserve. My father was born in a tipi near Chief Mountain, back when we Stoneys used to roam up and down along the foothills freely, from Montana north into Alberta. Along that route there were ranches that used to hire us Indians regularly, so that's where I thought our family group should settle.

"When I spoke to my family and elders they agreed with me and said I should go to work on it, to see if we could get a small reserve of our own. But when I went to see the head chief of our tribe, he just laughed at me and said we Indians had already gotten our reserves long ago and that was it. But I went around and talked to others about my idea, including government officials. Years passed, winters and summers went by; many of our families kept working down south, earning a living on the different ranches, but staying in tents at borrowed places, having no real land of their own.

"Finally the federal government gave me an official answer to my letters and requests. They said, 'We cannot give you any of our crown land, because you already have your reserve next to Banff National Park. But we can allow from your trust money funds up to $500,000 with which you can buy a private ranch for your home.' In those days land was pretty cheap, so we didn't even need all that money in order to buy our Eden Valley Reserve, which has 2,000 acres. We moved here in 1950 and we all helped each other to build new houses, barns, toilets and so forth. Most of us camped outside in tents during the good weather, and some of us still do that today.

"Although we're not very far from our relatives back on the main reserve, there were no direct roads until just lately so we used to travel there by train through Calgary, the long way around. Those who wanted to ride by horseback could follow the same old trails used by our parents and forefathers. I've had to make this trip often, since the people usually elected me as their councillor and representative at tribal meetings.

"As councillor of my people I've watched carefully how we use our land and how our population is growing. As a result, I've bought several more pieces of land down this way with money from our tribal funds. You see, the ranch we originally bought for our reserve is fine for our homes, for some hunting and for grazing our livestock, but it doesn't grow grain or good hay. So I bought a place further out on the prairie where we could grow our own hay - two of our families have homes there and live on it. We are like our Hutterite neighbors, (a religious group originally from Europe) in that we try to work hard and support ourselves. Of course, lately we also make a good income from oil and gas royalties that big companies are paying for our land back on the main reserve. From that, each of us gets $400 per month, although we cannot say how long that will last."

While Johnny was talking to us, his wife finished her work, then stood quietly in the background for a while, finally saying a few words in Stoney. Johnny just kept talking, but I sensed he was being distracted. It turned out she was trying to rush him, as they still had to make a long drive to town for groceries to supply their camp. Like a typical old time Indian man, he talked until *he* felt it was time to go, at which point he said upon rising, "Well, we have other business to attend," then excused himself and drove off with his wife in a brand new shiny pickup truck.

Since my sister's tipi was not yet set up, we accepted Johnny's invitation and pitched our tent next to his. He was a friendly host, as I woke up in the middle of the night to hear him giving the same invitation to someone else, whose motor was running while headlights illuminated the inside of our tent. I heard Johnny saying, "The fellow in this little tent walked over here with his boy, *clear* across the mountains from B.C."

The next morning Beverly and Star arrived with our truck and more camping gear, including a new little tipi they had made as a surprise for Okan. They were quite disappointed when I said there were no poles available for it; there'd been very few poles in the camp and all of them now held up tipis. But when my sister heard about this she went off and soon located a set of small ones that were just right.

For the next few days we had a fine time visiting with friends in the tipi camp and at the nearby rodeo. At night we put on our dance clothes and enjoyed the beat of the drums. Many people came up and shook our hands, wanting to know something about our walk. Johnny told us that he crossed the mountains by that same route just once, but his forefathers had done it all the time. As a young guide, many years ago, he'd led an adventurous and rich easterner to some of the old Indian campsites and other scenic spots around this part of the Rocky Mountains.

During the main night of dancing, the gathering was told by announcer Roy Coyote to look from the dance arbour towards the west at a beautiful orange sunset which made the mountains stand out as dark silhouettes. It was easy to see our pass, so the announcer explained that my son and I had walked to the camp through there. Then he asked us for an "exhibition dance," a form of honor which allowed us to pick our own drum group and song, then have the whole dance floor to ourselves. By the time we finished, many people had gone out onto the floor and put money in a pile, which was then presented to us. Said the humorous Roy Coyote, "They don't want you two to have to walk back home again!"

32.

Standing Up For Nature

It's hard to believe when I think about it, but enough time has passed since our mountain walk that my little companion is now several inches taller than his dad, and at the moment spending his third fall season as a guide up along those same wild Rocky Mountain crags and slopes, getting to know country I'll probably never visit. Our Swiss forefathers would be proud to see this incarnation of their transplanted mountain genes. His Blackfoot forefathers would be pleased to see that their profound love for animals and nature is being carried on.

But even in those remote wilderness areas my son is faced with a moral dilemma: The animals he so loves and respects are being shot by those who can afford the money so they can take back their hides and horns as trophies in homes that are far away. He knows all the arguments in favor of these adventures, and he also respects feelings that are against them. But right now he needs to earn money for his further schooling, and he finds it amazing to be paid well while getting to roam in the wilderness terrain that is for most just a dream, or at best, a vacation.

Wilderness of the kind still found in the heights of the Rockies is so rare today that few of us ever experience it first hand. Yet in spite of that, there are people wanting to disturb still more of it, especially now that machinery will allow them to dig up and cut down natural resources in the most difficult locations. But with darned near everything already disturbed wherever we go in our daily lives, has not the time come to bring an end to any more of this? Should not all remaining pure wilderness be left that way, as a bridge between modern society and our natural past?

Sometimes I get discouraged, thinking that maybe it really doesn't matter anymore. We've already gone too far, and soon there will be way more important concerns totally beyond our control. Nature has always managed to correct its mistakes, and

right now we seem to be the biggest mistake of all. The issue of
our world's population explosion is enough to back my pessi-
mism; no species has ever escaped the wrath of nature if it becomes too numerous. Famine and disease have been the common corrective measures.

Our dilemma with nature requires radical change in the ways
of humankind, yet where are the leaders who will take us through
them? Even if there were humans wise enough to think of ways,
our pessimistic society would never accept them. We'll do the
same with this as we do to all government leaders: We wail and
cry, saying they lack honesty and vision. Yet, when a visionary
person steps forward we encourage our media to attack them
mercilessly, until they can find us some shred of evidence as to
why we should dislike them, after which we all turn on them. As
a result, we've been ending up with the kind of leaders we de-
serve....

Here, in this part of the Rocky Mountains, we've recently held
some round-table meetings among local people regarding major
questions about land and nature. Instead of relying on political
leaders to make decisions for us from far away, we tried to agree
on solutions among ourselves. The experiment wasn't totally
successful, but it was a step in the right direction for a populace
that has too long allowed wealth and politics to direct the future
of their environment. At the round-table were loggers, miners,
tourist promoters, and of course many staunch nature lovers,
each rightly wanting to be considered in any decisions made
about how to treat our part of the world.

No one came to this round-table with a name card saying
"Environmentalist," though you might have expected quite a
few at such a hearing. I'm hoping the reason for this was that
our society is finally coming to realize that we must *all* be envi-
ronmentalists. Various speakers at the table, in one way or another, said this. By now we know that the health of our world's environment is truly in danger. It wasn't too many years ago that
even American presidents still publicly doubted it.

As in all major discussions between various kinds of people,
there was posturing and jockeying for position among the vari-

ous sectors at this round-table. It reminded me of how the rest of the crowded world operates on a daily basis - someone is always trying to get just a little more for themselves, and no one ever seems fully satisfied. One minute, ranchers and hunters became allies against tourist developers, while trying to protect their favorite wilderness places, next they battled with each other about whether those with guns should be allowed to enter areas fenced off for cattle, or whether cows should be allowed to go where there are animals for hunting. Change the issues and it's the same everywhere: Too many people, each wanting things their own way. Here, we argued with words at a round-table; in Bosnia and Rwanda they do it outside, with weapons.

The aftermath of our round-table discussion was even more discouraging. Using big maps, we had managed to reach some general agreements, as shown by various colors indicating future uses and non-uses for various parts of our region. That meant some pristine wilderness areas would no longer be open to tree cutting or mineral extractions, while other parts would be more available for general uses. As soon as these agreements were announced to the public, there was a huge outcry, as most everyone found some item they didn't like and used it to condemn the whole process.

Especially vocal were those employed in the "resource extraction" sector - loggers and miners who insisted that society owed them the right to make their livelihood wherever necessary, claiming there is too much undeveloped park land already. It seems to me that only someone without children could voice that opinion, since an expanding population makes such lands ever more of a premium.

"Preserving nature costs jobs," has become a common battlecry among many working folks, who use the image of an empty dinner plate to symbolize what the further preservation of natural places would mean for them and their kids. Yet, the truth is that ever-larger machines, bought by ever-larger companies, make ever-less people needed to strip ever-greater chunks of remaining nature. The person who doesn't see that, needs to have something more than an eye checkup....

But where were all these critics and complainers when the round-table sessions were being held? The meetings were well publicized, everyone was welcome, and all were given a chance to speak up. Some said they were unable to come because of work, yet that's the way of democracy; you can pick your own priorities, and you can grumble afterwards when you missed out on some important options.

The young of today seem far more actively interested in our world's environment, so there's still hope that they pick up on that round-table experience and develop it. They know that the challenges ahead will be much greater; maybe they'll learn from our mistakes and misplaced priorities that have brought us so close to environmental disaster.

When I left city life over twenty-five years ago and moved into the wilderness, I figured to leave behind such discussions, and to avoid debates like this. I preferred to let others argue and get mad. But now I realize that one day those "others" could be the ones to show up here at my doorstep and tell me something they've decided, and it might be a decision about my homeland that I won't like. Then they'll remind me that I didn't bother coming around while they were democratically working to decide it. So I urge each and every one of you most strongly: If you want to live in Harmony with Nature - wherever you are - you'll have to continually stand up for it. Don't wait too long, or there may not be enough Nature left to stand up for!